THE PARENT ENTREPRENEUR

How to cope with starting and running a business as a parent.

TERRY CHIU

Published by Venture Motion Publishing
First Edition 2019
ISBN 978-1-9162395-0-0

CONTENTS

FOREWORD

Perhaps two of the most challenging things in modern life are running a business and parenting. The parent entrepreneur is a special breed of human, balancing the risks of starting a business whilst raising little humans at the same time. If dealing with porridge being dashed across the room, chaotic scenes of planking tantrums in the middle of the supermarket, or the smell of vomit following you around isn't enough, you go and quit your stable 9 to 5 job and risk everything to follow a life of balancing cashflow, the stress of managing both customers and staff, not to mention the loneliness of running a business.

Being a parent entrepreneur is one of the toughest yet most rewarding roles you can take on, and it's for anyone who wants to build a better life for themselves and their family. I have started, operated, invested in, failed, made money and sold businesses across a broad range of industries, including ecommerce, property, professional services, consulting, digital marketing, technology, health and beauty, and even pharmaceutical industries. I have a wife and two young kids, and I operate all my business activities around this crazy family life that I'm sure you're familiar with.

Throughout the years, I've navigated through the maze of balancing a fast-paced business life with trying to be a good parent to the best of my abilities. There have been many low and challenging points throughout this journey, but ultimately there have been some very rewarding and happy times.

There are plenty of good parenting books and plenty of informative business books that can give you step by step 'how to' guides for both parenting and business. This is not one of those books. Instead I wanted to use my knowledge and experience of being a parent in business to take you through my journey, and how to cope with starting and running a business, cope with being a parent, and how it's possible to balance both.

Kids grow up so quickly that if you blink you'll miss another milestone. I didn't want to miss seeing my kids grow up just because of my business ambitions, so I build and structure all my businesses around this ideal. It's tough, but it is totally possible to be a parent and still have an ambitious business career – and still keep your sanity!

I didn't start with plenty of resources, money or people around me to help build something. I started just like every other parent, trying to build a better life for my family through starting and running my own business. And so can you!

Section One

PLANNING YOUR BUSINESS

1

STARTING A BUSINESS WITH A FAMILY

Trying to start a business is difficult in itself, but when you are trying to do it whilst raising a family, especially when you have young kids, that takes a whole extra level of commitment. Every parent knows that raising young kids takes a lot of time, attention and patience. Many parents will recall those sleepless nights when the little ones are waking up because they had a bad dream or simply want to sneak into your bed. Then there are the times when they simply don't want to comply with your instructions and lie down in the middle of the supermarket floor. Or they kick off, scream and cry because they don't want to wear their own shoes, they want to wear yours instead.

It can be both physically and emotionally draining simply being a parent, so the last thing you want to do when you get in from work, with your kids screaming and refusing to eat their dinner or go to bed, is to spend a few more hours in the evening hunched up at a desk to work on your business plans.

QUICK STORY

When we had our first child Natasha, I had already been in business for a number of years. At the time, I ran a digital marketing agency with my former business partner. We had a team of 15 staff and strong sales revenue approaching seven figures, so we already had a decent foundation in business.

But when I sold my share of the business and went on to start a new consultancy and tech start-up on my own, I had to start again from the beginning. At the same time, my wife became pregnant with our son, Jamie. I had gone from the relatively stable and comfortable life of running a successful digital marketing agency with a business partner and strong team of 15 to support me, to starting a brand new consulting business and tech start-up from the ground up, with just a handful of staff.

The new digital consultancy business was high level and involved a lot of me personally going out to see clients while the team worked on projects in the background. The tech start-up was an app, which connected people's hidden talents and skills to others who were looking to solve everyday practical problems. It was originally intended to be a just small side hustle alongside the consultancy but somehow I had managed to raise £250,000 from an investor, so the app became a business in its own right and I had to hire a small team to help me run that too.

I was now back at square one, working on the day-to-day operations, managing staff, working on clients myself. Not only was I running a digital consultancy business, I was now building a start-up on the side with an investor wanting to see results. The investment gave us a 24-month runway to make the app bring in revenue. Loosely translated, the investment that we had would last for 24 months and if the app didn't start to build some kind of revenue by month 18 we were in trouble.

It was tough, the pressure was on and I was in the thick of it. I tried to find ways to balance my workload between the consultancy and the start-up, and I found myself working the longest hours I had ever worked. I was used to long hours but this time I had a wife and daughter to care for. I've never felt a level of stress like it.

When you're a single adult or a couple without kids, if you earn less you just cut back. You can't do that when you have a family, you have try to maintain their way of life, it's not their fault you decided to start again, it's not their fault that you walked away from the previous business because you wanted a new challenge, it's not their fault you may have just taken on more than you can chew. I probably only slept a few hours each night - I was too highly strung and stressed to have a good night's sleep.

But this is where the training starts and what prepares you for a gruelling first 12 months in business.

In the previous agency, we had got to a point where my business partner and I were running the business at a high level, and not necessarily getting involved in the day-to-day operations. But now I had to be much more hands on and I was burning myself out. Then, one week I got very ill.

It's strange how stress can show in different ways in different people. I felt enormous pressure to present a strong front – I had to. I now had a small team, I had clients, investors and my family all depending on just me. The decisions I made on a daily basis would make a difference to their lives. I felt like I'd taken on too much. I felt stretched, alone and under a great deal of strain. I tried to shield the stress and worry from my family, but my wife Yan could feel how stressed I was and worried that I was making myself ill. My daughter Natasha was still very young and needed attention from her dad. I was working 15 hours every day. I was drinking a lot in the evening to numb the stress and to relax, and that too was taking a toll.

Getting in the Right Frame of Mind

When you're running your own business it becomes your entire life. It can become so overbearing that if you don't control your thoughts they will totally consume you. The lines between business and family can blur very quickly, and before you know it you can't tell the difference between family time and business time.

I've always paid a degree of attention to self help books and articles, and though I never fully embraced them, I researched enough to get me in the right frame of mind. I also watched videos on YouTube about techniques to control my way of thinking, and to help me gain some perspective on how I reacted to challenges. Over time, as I got into running both businesses, I learnt how to regulate my emotions, better control my thoughts, and also how to improve the way I responded to pressured situations.

> **THE MOST IMPORTANT THING TO DO IS TO TRAIN YOUR BRAIN TO SWITCH MODES.**

What I gradually learnt was how to separate my work thoughts, stresses and concerns from my family thoughts. It was like my brain was a box filled with all my thoughts of business, family and life mixed together. Then over time, I learnt to split these thoughts into completely different boxes for business and family. I learnt to close the business box whenever I was with my family and only open the family box. It wasn't always as clean cut as that, but it certainly trained me to prevent the stresses of running a business from spilling over into my family life.

2

WHY DO YOU WANT TO START A BUSINESS?

Starting a business is a big commitment. It's not just a change of job, it's a life-changing experience. It doesn't just affect you, it can affect your family and everyone else in your life too. With that in mind, you need to be completely honest with yourself about why you are starting your own business, because the answer to that question should be your complete focus and goal.

People often say, 'I want to be the boss', 'I don't want to answer to anyone anymore' or 'I don't want to make *my boss* rich anymore, *I* want to be rich'. There are so many reasons for starting a business, but many people who dive head first into starting a business never really think about their real reasons for taking that leap of faith.

> **"THE REASON YOU GO INTO BUSINESS IS REALLY IMPORTANT BECAUSE IT SETS THE TONE AND GOAL FOR YOUR JOURNEY AS A BUSINESS OWNER."**

It doesn't matter what your reason is, but it has to be something you really believe in, because when times get tough, and inevitably at some point they will get tough, your true reason for starting your business will give you strength and keep you focused.

Not answering to anyone

Starting a business gives you the power to decide what direction you want to go in. What it doesn't give you is the ultimate freedom of not having to answer to someone else and there's a subtle difference. If you don't want to answer to anyone, starting a business isn't really the way forward.

When I started my first business, I realised that I had escaped from the daily instructions of one manager or boss, but I had acquired a whole new set of bosses – clients. Not only did I now have more than one boss, but my clients had no problem in ditching me if I made mistakes or didn't deliver. When you're employed, you have the safety net of employment law to make sure you don't just get fired on the spot. But when you have customers and clients, and you don't deliver, you're gone.

If you have investors in your business you have to answer to them too, and deliver the returns you promised, just like you had to deliver when you were employed and had a boss, but without the extra cushioning.

So here's the problem: many people are thinking about this 'boss' thing the wrong way. They are trying to escape being told what to do by the boss, and when they start getting customers or investors they realise that they haven't escaped that feeling at all.

I've run client service-based businesses in different forms since 2006 and I quickly realised that having clients meant I had even more people to answer to. Running your own business isn't about having a boss or not, it's about having the freedom to make your own decisions. It's not about whether you're being told what to do or not, it's about creating a product or service and turning it into a business, and ultimately making decisions that steer you closer to the real reason why you started a business in the first place.

Starting your own business is not so much about being your own boss, it's more about having the freedom to choose who you work with. It enables you to make the decisions that have to be made to help that business thrive. You might have new bosses in the form of customers and clients, but it's up to you to decide who you work with, which projects to pursue, and ultimately which direction you want your business to take.

Getting rich

If you're thinking of starting your own business, it's highly likely you'll have thought about the money that comes with it. Let's be honest, a big part of starting your own business is the potential to earn significantly more than you were earning working for somebody else. Money is important and so it should be. You're taking a risk leaving your comfortable job and lifestyle so it's only right to reap the financial rewards from all the stress, hard work and risk.

Let's say you've taken the leap of faith and started your business. You've gone through all the highs and lows of building it, the money starts flowing in and you're back to more than comfortable. Will the extra zeros make all the difference? Of course earning more money could change your life, but is that all it will do? Is there more to it than just the money? What does your business *mean* to you?

Throughout my business journey I've worked with people at every stage of business. Some were just starting out and scraping by to keep their fledgling start-ups in business. Others, at the other end of spectrum, had successful businesses or even groups of companies. Over the years many of these successful entrepreneurs have not just become clients or investors, they've become close friends. Nearly all of them say that after a certain level of wealth, the money starts to mean something else. A common theme from some of my successful clients and investors, is that once your business reaches a certain level of autonomy, where you have teams and departments looking after finances and profitability, you stop looking at the money. Instead they focus on legacy and what difference the business makes to a wider group of people; their own family, to the people who work there, to local community and even to society in general.

What I take from this is that money is an important tool and enabler.

> **MONEY ALLOWS YOU TO SURVIVE, GROW AND REACH YOUR GOALS, BUT THE ACTUAL GOAL ISN'T THE MONEY.**

The money just enables you to reach that goal. In the beginning you might not know exactly what your purpose in business is, and although it might seem like it's money right now, it certainly won't be when you have accumulated enough of it.

Having clear goals

In reality, being your own boss and not having to answer to anyone, or accumulating money and wealth, are stepping stones to your real purpose for starting your own business.

Leaving your stable 9 to 5 job and being your own boss gives you the freedom to make the decisions needed to build and scale your business. Once your business is steady and you begin to scale up, the cash starts to flow in and you become stable and comfortable. The money then enables you to do other things, like grow your business, start other businesses, help others start their business by investing in them, or help communities or charities. Ultimately, the reason for starting your own business will be a combination of these things, but the purpose and end goal will always be much bigger than that.

Think about the difference you will make to other people, to society, to your industry or to your own family. Is that the real reason you're starting your own business? To help and make a difference to others? Perhaps you feel your industry needs to be better, so you bring out a better product to improve it? Perhaps it's to make a difference to your local community or even to society, and improve people's lives?

Whatever the real reason you are starting your own business, make sure you are honest with yourself and that your purpose is much bigger than just the money. In tough times, this reason will keep you focused and see you through.

QUICK STORY

When my daughter was born, I was running the digital marketing agency with my former business partner. As a client services business, client communication was important. Even though we had a team helping us manage clients, and my business partner was back at the office, some of our bigger clients still wanted to liaise with a specific director. When you're running your own business there's no such thing as paternity leave, you just have to try and juggle everything.

My wife was in hospital and ready to go into labour. I was by her side, but found myself in a situation where for part of it, I had to deal with a client emergency. Although the business was doing well, I didn't have the freedom to just drop everything. I realised at that point in time that no matter how well the business was doing revenue-wise, money wasn't what was most important.

Take some time to think about this. If money wasn't a worry and life was comfortable. What would you like to do, and who would you like to do it with? Be totally honest with yourself. Peel back the layers in your mind and think about what you'd really like to do in life. It might not come to you straight away, and it might take some time to discover the real answer, but whatever you come up with, that's the real reason you want to start a business.

3

STARTING A BUSINESS WITH A 9 TO 5 JOB

Being a parent means many things, but the most important and fundamental role is, of course, being able to provide for your family. Starting a business is a big decision, one that won't just affect you, but will ultimately have an impact on your family and their life too. Before you take that leap of faith and start up on your own, it's important to make sure that you triple plan and triple check everything. That means *everything* – your business plan, sales forecasts, marketing. Make sure you're not just scraping by to put food on the table.

Don't give up the day job…yet!

Before making that big jump into the world of business, the safest thing to do is keep your job for as long as possible, and work around it to get your business close to, if not off, the ground. This means sacrificing a whole heap of stuff to make time to work on your business – before and after work, before your kids are up and after your kids are in bed, and even at the weekends. Any bit of spare time that isn't your 9 to 5 job, or your family time, should be spent on your business if you are serious about starting a business in the safest possible way. Stop all hobbies and any extra curricular activities for now until you have made some progress. If you usually have some kind of activity that you've committed to, such as the gym or a sport, try to cut it down as much as possible so you can focus on planning your business while you still have an income from your full-time job.

Having a 9 to 5 job and working on your business is like working two jobs. Get up a few hours earlier than you usually would and set aside time to work on your business in the morning if you can. In the evening, after the kids are in bed, get straight back to work on your business. Just think, even if you can fit in two hours in the morning and in the evening, that's four hours per day. During the week that's 20 extra hours you've managed to squeeze out of the weekdays, and that's not including weekends.

Of course, if you are a parent you can't sacrifice that precious time at the weekends with your kids. Take the weekend as your cheat days and rest days (if you can call it rest with kids!). But that's not to say you should take the whole weekend as rest. If you can, you should get back to working on your business as soon as the kids are in bed. If you can match the extra hours you managed to squeeze from your working week, that's another eight hours at the weekend, bringing the total number of hours per week to 28 spent on your business, and that's not pushing it too much. It means you can still get some sleep (as much as you can with kids) and still have *some* recreational time during the weekends with your family.

Making the most of 'dead time'

As well as those allocated hours throughout the week, utilise any 'dead time' you have to do some non-core activities, such as brainstorming, jotting down notes, and planning things in your head. Use your phone to note things down and save ideas as and when they come to you. Depending on how you get to work, the travel time can also be used to plan your business. If you drive to work, use the voice recording app on your phone to record ideas for later. I sometimes use a dictation app that transcribes my voice into notes, which I can review and edit later. In fact, some of this book was written using the voice app and transcribed afterwards, which helped me get words on the page when I was on long motorway drives. If you are on a train or bus, that's even better because it means you can type things out into a notes app. You absolutely don't need to be at a desk to be productive.

> **GET INTO A HABIT OF UTILISING 'DEAD TIME' AND MAKING IT PRODUCTIVE.**

Without wishing to sound crude, I once wrote the entire framework for a new business idea whilst I was on the toilet. It was the only place I could get some peace and quiet while my two year old was hunting me down to cover me in lipstick and dress me up in wigs! My point is, not everything needs to be done at a desk. A lot of foundational thinking and brainstorming can be done wherever you are. Sometimes the best ideas come to you in the most unusual circumstances. These days my wife is used to me just whipping out my phone in the most unlikely places when an idea comes to me. It's not uncommon for me to be typing notes in my phone during a nappy change – for my son, not me!

The side hustle

The side hustle is an important step to starting a business. It's a way for you to step into the world of business without leaping in. It enables you to start a business with the cushion and security of having a wage to fall back on if it doesn't work out. Side hustles are quite common nowadays, but back when I started people had one job and that was enough.

Before I started my first proper business I was in marketing for a mobile phone distribution company. I say 'proper' first business because I had several side businesses as a teenager - bootleg games, selling mobile phones, and other things I sourced online.

Working in marketing at the mobile company really helped step up both my marketing and side hustle game. During the years I worked there I developed a strong understanding of marketing within a fast-paced environment, and made quite a few important contacts that I would later call back on in my career.

I would learn and expand my knowledge of marketing in the evenings on top of my real world experience, and over time I not only became good at my marketing job within the company, but also learnt about wider marketing techniques outside of my job. I now had enough experience in marketing to take on side hustles in marketing itself.

A side hustle often starts with something that you're already experienced in, perhaps even the industry that you're already working in, and you feel you have more to offer to enhance the service or product. It goes without saying that you have to be careful to make sure you're not doing anything that contradicts your employment contract. In many cases, your side hustle might be born out of a hobby and you've figured out a way for it to make money.

QUICK STORY

One of my side hustles started in my early twenties when a friend introduced me to his brother-in-law, who wanted to start a hot tub company and needed a website and marketing literature. I had gathered enough expertise from my degree and some basic self-taught website coding to be able to put together a website. I had also learnt enough about design and Photoshop over the years to churn out a reasonable business card and brochure. I had less of an idea of how to price the job, but as it was my first proper marketing project I charged him by the hour. That first project netted me £700 and I was over the moon! I had suddenly become a freelancer.

Then the thought occurred to me – this one client had paid me £700 for a basic project, but if I could get 10 clients a month I'd be making £7,000 - £10,000 a month. That really put the £18,000 salary from my marketing job at the time into perspective. I took on a few more projects and was making good money as a side hustle when I decided to take the leap of faith of going freelance full time. Before making the big move I did some market research of my own. I called up all the local marketing agencies under my position at the company I was working for to ask for brochures, day rates and anything I could get hold of to understand more about what these big agencies were charging and how I could stand out as a freelancer.

I spent the evenings and weekends strengthening my business plan. Coming up with ideas for how to get new clients of my own, and putting my service offering together. I spent those evenings designing my brochures and website. I had enough information, experience and confidence given to me from my freelance projects to take the next step – I handed in my notice. For the first time in my life, my side hustle became my main hustle.

All that planning will pay off

It can be daunting making that big jump into starting your own business. From that point on, you won't have a regular monthly wage to rely on. If you're going to put food on the table, you have to go out and earn it. But all those evenings and weekends that you sacrifice now in planning and quietly building your business will pay off. You will be ready to go out and get your own business, and not waste time on further planning. You will know exactly what you need to do on day one.

Nowadays, I'm involved in running several businesses but I'm still constantly coming up with new business ideas. Even though I could test them out in my day-to-day business time, they all still start as a side hustle. I still work on these new ideas in my own time, in the evenings and in the mornings, until I build some kind of traction and I allocate more time and resources to them. It's important never to lose that side hustle mentality, because it keeps things exciting and it trains you to be constantly creative.

4

IS STARTING A BUSINESS RIGHT FOR YOU?

You want to start your own business. You're also a parent and you have to maintain a day job before your business starts to build momentum, so you can maintain your family's lifestyle. After a long day at work you come home to absolute chaos. The kids are ratty because they are tired, the house is a mess, you rush through dinner, homework and get the kids into the bath, and if you're *really* lucky they fall asleep straight away. You're mentally and physically drained and you can barely conjure up the energy to have a proper conversation with your partner. Sound familiar?

Here's the thing, if you're going to start, survive and grow in business, there is one thing that you will need to master. *Sacrifice.* It could be sacrificing your hobbies, social life, sleep or even time with your family. It's up to you what you sacrifice and what you prioritise. But something's going to have to give for you to be able to get your business off the ground. When you're thinking about your business idea, if it doesn't make you instantly wake up, bounce out of bed or the sofa and get you super excited, it's important to examine the reasons why.

Do you believe in your business?

You have to be honest with yourself about how confident you are with your business idea before you take those first steps. You have to be pretty certain there is a market out there for your product or service and how you can pull it off. Ask yourself this:

'If I was my target customer, would I HONESTLY *buy the product or services that I want to offer?'*

If the answer is not a resounding 'YES!', with absolutely no hesitation, then you have to ask yourself why you wouldn't. Go back to the drawing board, refine and tweak your product or service until you get that definitive answer. You'll know that your idea is perfect when you feel the adrenaline pumping through your body, the tingling sensation and the goosebumps that you get just thinking it.

Are you an intrapreneur or an entrepreneur?

An intrapreneur is a person who works for an employer and shows entrepreneurial skills, but may not necessarily want to take on the risk of starting their own business. An intrapreneur takes on the responsibility of innovating new ideas, products and processes, or any new invention within the organisation

Perhaps you are a natural intrapreneur, but not an entrepreneur. You may already have a day job that pays well, is stable and has some gradual career development opportunities, and you actually quite enjoy it. Perhaps you're considering starting your own business because you think that might lead to a better life for you and your family, but your current life isn't actually that bad at all, and in fact you're in a pretty comfortable position.

If you only half think that starting a business might give you a better life, but at the same time you think your current life is pretty good, you have to ask yourself whether you'd be better off staying in your job, excelling at it and climbing that career ladder, rather than risking it to start up on your own.

QUICK STORY

I often get friends and associates asking me for advice when they are thinking of starting a business. One friend in particular was a senior manager at the company he worked at - he was on a good salary, with a company car and a pension. He had two kids and a wife, and he had a pretty good life, but he was thinking of going it alone. He would have had to start from the bottom to find his own clients, establish a new team and perhaps spend the first few years living on a lean budget.

We did a lot of soul searching and we concluded that he just didn't have it in him to start from scratch. He admitted that he enjoyed his job and the lifestyle that he and his family were living. He had plenty of ideas about how he could make his consultancy services better and that's why he wanted to start his own business. He had an entrepreneurial itch that he needed to scratch, and he thought that starting his own business would satisfy that itch. However, he wasn't willing to give up and sacrifice what he had at the time.

Instead, what we came up with was a business plan for the company he worked at. This would allow him to start a new division and team, implement his new plans, increase revenue for the company and be rewarded for his ideas. We recognised that he was an intrapreneur not an entrepreneur.

An entrepreneur loves risk and is willing to sacrifice and start from the bottom to achieve their ultimate goals. They constantly have new ideas to disrupt the market, and they have the energy to try to make something work even if they are tired. They don't care if something fails, they just keep bouncing back. An intrapreneur also has fresh ideas, energy and a strong work ethic, but isn't willing to sacrifice what they have now.

Figure out if you are an entrepreneur or intrapreneur by asking yourself these questions:

- **Am I willing to sacrifice my standard of living right now for a potentially better life in the future?** If not, you're more of an intrapreneur.
- **Do I have the energy and time to be able to pull off starting my own business, or am I going to be more successful pitching my idea to my boss, with some backing and stability?** If you're not willing to make or find the time to get your business off the ground, but you have the ideas and work ethic, then being an intrapreneur might suit you more.
- **Do I really want to start a business, or do I just want to just grow in my career?** If you think that you would do better in growing your career and excelling at it, you're more of an intrapreneur.

Are you prepared to disrupt normal family life?

Although you may be fired up and ready to go into business, is your family on the same page? Whatever line of business you decide to go into, at some stage there will be some level of change and disruption to normal family life.

Starting a new business most certainly means some sacrifices in the initial years. Some of those sacrifices may come from spending less time with your family or not being able to participate in some normal family activities as much as you're used to. Perhaps you may need to be away from home more and your partner may have to look after the kids by themselves more often. Whilst *you* may be prepared to do this, what effect will this have on your partner, kids and family?

Communication is the key here. By bringing your family on board and taking them through your goals, what you hope to achieve and your timeline, it can prepare them for what's coming and what kind of changes and disruptions to expect.

Do some soul searching

Over the years, I've learnt that you have to constantly test yourself and your business idea. You have to routinely do some soul searching to find out how much you're willing to sacrifice to get your business idea off the ground, or to the next level if you've already started.

You also have to constantly refine, tweak and improve your products and services. While they may have been perfect when you first started, as time goes on, your competitors improve their products too. You need to ensure that yours remains a perfect concept in which you feel 100 per cent confident.

Starting a business, particularly with kids and a family, is a very steep climb. It takes a lot of energy, stamina and a tiny sprinkle of craziness to turn your idea into a viable business. You'll need to be prepared to sacrifice a few things, and in many cases that might even include sleep! Make sure you feel the sacrifice will be worth it.

5

CHOOSING THE RIGHT BUSINESS MODEL FOR YOU

Figuring out why you want to start a business is important, but so is understanding what kind of business you're suited to and will be good at. Over the course of my business career I have started many types of businesses – most of them I invested a lot of time and money into. Some failed and others morphed into the businesses that I have today. It's taken a lot of trial and error to gauge what type of business model works best for me. To succeed in business, it's not enough figuring out what type of business you want to start. You also need to figure out how the business model suits your skill set, personality and family circumstances.

Know yourself

In order to work out the type of business model that will work for you, be honest with yourself about what kind of business models are likely to suit your personality and skill set the most. What are your strengths and weaknesses? Are you better suited to high volume, low margin business models, where you sell products and services en masse, but earn less on each sale? Or do you prefer low volume but highly customised products and services, where you can charge higher prices and make higher margins, but require a lot more effort.

Even from a very young age, I could see the difference in my children's predispositions when it comes to quality vs quantity. My daughter is a perfectionist, she likes everything in an orderly fashion. She doesn't need a lot of toys but what she does have needs to be perfect, neat and tidy – she demands quality. My son, on the other hand, doesn't care so much about quality, he just wants quantity. He wants lots of everything and doesn't care what condition these things are in, as long as he has plenty of them. Even when it comes to food preferences, these traits are clear. My daughter would rather have a small bowl of very high quality ice cream than lots of average quality ice cream, yet my son doesn't care what he eats as long as there's lots of it. I can already see how they will operate as adults, and what kind of tasks or work would best suit their characters.

When planning a business model, it's essential you're honest with yourself about the type of personality you have and how this will translate into a successful business that suits who you are and plays to your strengths.

QUICK STORY

One thing I realised after years of trying out different models was that, for me, the ones that succeeded seemed to be high ticket products and services. They were business models that required a lot of my time and attention, but allowed me to charge a high price for my products and services. My consulting, technology development and property development businesses all involved high price, high margins but low volume transactions. They required attention to detail, with a customised approach to how deals were done, and how the product or service was delivered. I found that I was good at marketing and selling these high ticket products where it wasn't done at scale, and where I could tailor the way I marketed and sold it to the customer.

I had tried to start businesses where the margins were much lower but it was easier to sell them in volume with much less effort on my part. One such model came in my early business career, when mobile phones weren't as sophisticated as today's smartphones, but were starting to get more functionally such as cameras and video recording. I had discovered a service where you could back-up your phone remotely through the internet without any cables. At the time, this service was relatively high-tech and sold on a low-priced subscription basis. I would buy the service from the provider, white label it and sell it under my own brand. After taking away costs, I would earn just £1.50 per month per user. Once I got a subscriber on board there was nothing more I needed to do. As long as the subscriber continued with the service, I would keep getting the commission payments. Although it was a low margin product it was relatively easy to sign up hundreds of subscribers in a short space of time. The problem was there was no way for me to enhance or tailor the product and no way for me to offer better customer service at that scale and charge more. The high volume model just didn't suit my character.

A business model that will work around your family

Although in the early years of starting a business there may be some changes in your family life and the amount of time you spend with your family, in the long-term your business has to work alongside normal family life too. Choosing a business model that will eventually fit well with your family life can make the whole experience of running a business much easier.

Starting something from home is the ideal way to merge business and family life. If you are passionate about baking for example, you could start a custom cake business where you do the baking at home around family time, and sell your cakes to your local community.

QUICK STORY

My wife loves crochet and knitting, and when she was pregnant with our daughter she started knitting unique baby items for her. Some of her friends asked if she would knit something for their own children too if they paid for the wool and her time. Realising she could do this around being a mother at home, she started taking orders. I built a website for her and she starting posting on Facebook and Instagram. Word spread and a few more orders came in. Before she knew it, she had a side business she could operate around the kids.

It was a lifestyle business that fitted around her own schedule as a mum rather than fitting family around her business.

But even if your business can't be operated from home, think about how you can tweak or tailor your business idea to suit family life. For example, if you are starting a restaurant, café or retail shop and have to be away from home for big parts of the day, are you able to take the kids to work with you? Perhaps you could put something in the shop that could entertain them whilst they are with you at work, and better still get them involved in the business.

6

STICK WITH WHAT YOU KNOW

The world is full of business opportunities. Everywhere you look, there are literally a million ways that you can make money. If you are thinking of starting a business, everything may look like a great business idea. The reality is not everything will be for you.

One thing I've learnt in business is that the money doesn't matter nearly as much as you think it does right now. You can literally make money any way, anywhere and anyhow, but at some point during your failures and successes you'll start to think about what it all means.

As a consultant, I've worked with lots of clients with different types of business models and I see how profitable certain business types actually are, and as an outside consultant, how they could become more profitable. When I'm out with friends, family or with clients, I usually spend some time looking at businesses and working out their business models. If I'm in a restaurant I often work out in my head how profitable that business is, what the overheads might look like, their staff costs, and how much margin there is in their meals. I grew up in the restaurant business so I know how restaurants generally operate and what kind of margins to expect.

If I'm in a retail store I try to work out how much it might cost to make or import that product, and how much their rent might cost. I was even at a pet shop once with my daughter and I had a long conversation with the owner about where he got all his livestock from, how much it cost to feed all the animals, and how quickly he needed to sell livestock to become profitable.

Turn your passion into success

If you do something you're good at, and feel passionate about, you will eventually find a way to make money with it. All types of businesses, no matter how exciting or mundane, can make money and scale, but success depends on what it all means to the business owner. What I'm trying to say here is that the money will eventually come, but when it does come, then what? What does your business actually mean to you?

If you have spent years training and refining a skill and you're passionate about it, then focus on that and become an expert in that field. Don't stretch yourself too thinly and become just okay at many things, even though it might seem that there's money to be made there. There is money to be made everywhere so you might as well do something that means something to you, and you're good at.

QUICK STORY

When I sold my share of the digital marketing agency that my former business partner and I started and grew together, I started a new digital consultancy of my own. At the same time I also started a little tech start-up called Gurooo. It was my first foray into the tech start-up world and it didn't last long.

The digital consultancy business was immediately a success because I had over ten years' experience in the marketing agency business at the time. It was a business I had lots of expertise in, and something I genuinely loved. With the tech start-up it was my first time raising seed investment and putting together a team to build and market an app.

In the consultancy business, most of the time I spent on clients was billable. I had spent the previous ten years programming my mind to think that all work had to be directly or indirectly generating revenue, or at least contain some kind of value that would contribute financially at some point. The tech start-up was a completely different way of working. We raised £250,000 in seed investment and it provided two years' runway for us to build and market our app idea. For those two years the app wouldn't make any money, but it would build up a user base to eventually make money much further down the line.

I didn't realise at the time, but my brain was not programmed to run a business like that and I couldn't make it work. The investment was pulled and we ran out of runway and time to keep developing the app. Meanwhile, the consultancy business was doing well. Through a client, we ended up selling the system built for Gurooo and I recouped some of the investment that I had ploughed in myself.

I genuinely believe that the consultancy business worked so well because I loved what I did and I was good at it.

When you're starting a business, play to your strengths and focus on something you already have experience in.

7

FUNDING YOUR START-UP BUSINESS

To accomplish anything in business you need one of two things; time or money. If you don't have enough time to accomplish something in your business then you need money to hire the people who can. If you don't have the money or capital to hire people, then you need to try to find the time to do it yourself, and if you don't know how to then you'll need to find the time to learn. Quite often it's a combination of both time *and* money, and figuring out which tasks need your attention and which ones can be delegated.

Before thinking about borrowing money to start a business, ask yourself whether you really need it. Most people think they need to raise capital in order to start a business, but the reality is that most of the time you can start something on a shoestring and slowly grow from there.

There are plenty of sources for start-up business funding, and whilst I won't cover them all in detail, here are some places to find start-up finance:

1. Your own savings This is the obvious first choice. Family members may also be able to help, but I would suggest trying not to borrow from friends. Friendship and money in my opinion can get messy. It's all fine when things are going well, but when things aren't going as planned in business, it can ruin a perfectly good friendship.

2. Your bank The most common external source of funding most people think of is their own bank. After all, you would think that through all these years banking with them, they would understand your financial situation better than anyone, right? The reality is, banks don't like lending to new businesses because most new businesses have a low rate of success and are risky. When your business has some trading history and operated for more than 12 months, there may be more finance options, but generally the bank is not a great source of funding when starting a new business.

3. Angel investors These are individuals or organisations who are willing to invest in your business because they can see potential in the idea. Usually, you will give them some equity in your business in exchange for their investment (how much equity will depend on your business, growth plans and what the investment consists of). Be careful about taking an investor's money, and make sure that you get as much legal advice to protect yourself so that you remain in control of your own business.

4. Local or national business grants You may be able to access local or national business grants, depending on the sector you are in. For example, certain cities may want to promote sustainability and there could be some special grants for green businesses.

5. No finance Depending on the type of business you start, you may not necessarily need any finance. I would suggest exploring all possible options and ways to start your business without borrowing any money or taking investment at the outset.

Bootstrapping

Bootstrapping is growing and starting your business as you run and work on it. It requires you to make money on day one, which you then plough back into the business to keep it growing and get you to the next stage. The main advantage to bootstrapping is that you are in complete control of the business and you make all the big decisions. If you have an investor with some equity in your business, you may have an agreement where you need to clear any big business decisions with them, and that can slow things down as they may not always agree with you.

Quite often when bootstrapping, you start with an MVP (Minimal Viable Product), a product or service that meets the minimum standard for you to be able to sell it. (Read more on MVPs, see chapter 13.) It will need continual improvement for it to become a great product or service, but it's good enough to start building some kind of revenue in the beginning.

The downside of bootstrapping is that growing your business can take more time, and every single decision you make is a balance between doing it for the short-term or the long-term. If you are reliant on everything you do in the business to bring in revenue, then most of these decisions will be short-term. When you're thinking of the long-term you need to do things that perhaps might not bring in revenue straight away, with a view to creating value for the future.

When you're bootstrapping, every decision you make and task you perform in the business needs to add value, whether it's measurable in the short-term or the long-term. Of course, bootstrapping all depends on the type of business you want to start. A service-based business is much easier to bootstrap, because generally you don't need to buy any stock upfront. If you are selling products or premises, you might need a small amount of capital to buy stock or rent premises in the first place.

QUICK STORY

When my former business partner and I grew our digital marketing agency, we bootstrapped the whole thing. We grew from just the two of us. He would bring in new clients and I would service them. Sometimes we didn't get paid properly, in fact that happened for a good couple of years in the beginning. After each new client, we would plough the money back into the business and hire more staff to service new clients.

In the early days of the agency, when we were about to land our first big client, there were seven of us working out of two tiny back rooms in someone else's offices. If we landed the deal it would become our biggest client account and change the dynamics of the agency. Before signing on the dotted line, the CEO wanted to see our offices. They certainly weren't fit to show the CEO of a big client! Across the hallway there was a much more spacious empty office– much more fitting for the type of agency we wanted to portray. We bribed the building reception with treats to let us borrow the space for a day for our big meeting. It was make or break – if we pulled this off we would land an account that would drastically increase our monthly revenue.

A day before the CEO visit, we kitted out the mock office with our desks, chairs, computers and printers. We even borrowed some friends within the building from other businesses that we'd become friendly with to help us fill out the much larger space, to make it look like we were a bigger and more established firm. It was very much a case of 'fake it until you make it'. In order to attract larger accounts, we had to give the right impression. The CEO already knew we could do the job, it was just a case of perception now.

After all our preparations, the CEO couldn't attend because of an emergency but signed with us anyway. That day became the day we went from simply bootstrapping to real business growth. That one deal enabled us to actually move into bigger offices, hire more staff and pitch to even bigger clients. A few years later, we managed to grow the business to near seven figures in revenue, and all from a bootstrapped business with no outside funding.

This showed me how growing a business is more about being resourceful and creative than it is about just having the funding.

When bootstrapping a new business, you have to consider whether your family circumstances will allow it. Bootstrapping will mean ploughing any spare cash straight back into your business and you should only pay yourself what you really need to survive. If you decide to go down the bootstrapping route, you should plan out and forecast your own family's cashflow, as well as how your partner can help cover family costs while you're building up the business. I cover more about this in chapter 18.

Funding checklist

Every business' situation is different and your situation will be different to mine. Depending on the type of business you want to start, here are some key questions to ask before getting any kind of finance or investment:

1. Are you able to produce an MVP (Minimal Viable Product) without any funding or investment?

2. Are you able to bring in some kind of revenue without funding?

3. Do you have any savings you can put in to start your business, even at the lowest level?

4. How long can your savings last without paying yourself anything?

5. Can your partner support the needs of the family while you are building revenue, or can a family member support you?

Bootstrapping can feel slow and requires a lot of discipline, but the business is yours and you are free to make the biggest decisions. With investment you get a capital boost at the beginning, but this often comes with more responsibilities and reporting. Sometimes when you're starting out, you just want to focus on running the business – all that extra reporting and managing investors can take its toll on your ability to focus and run the day-to-day operations.

8

BREAKING DOWN THE BIGGER PICTURE

Starting a business is exciting. You have this grand vision of one day realising your dream and becoming this huge success. You conjure up images and scenes from feel-good movies and overnight success stories that you read about from celebrity entrepreneurs. The truth is, those 'overnight' successes probably took years, if not decades, of hard work. Many people found out about the phenomenal success of Facebook creator Mark Zuckerberg, as billions of users started to connect through Facebook. In reality, Zuckerberg started Facebook many years before it became a mainstream success.

When thinking about and planning your new business, it's so easy to get sucked up into the hype of the big picture - that big dream when you first had the idea. In reality, that perfect vision of your successful business is way ahead in the future. On a day-to-day basis it can feel like an uphill struggle, and despite everything you do, that big picture still seems very far away.

Set yourself milestones

In order to feel like you're moving forward and getting closer to the big picture, it's helpful to break everything down into small manageable tasks and create milestones that are close to each other. Then break each milestone into a short series of tasks in order to reach the next milestone. This not only makes everything more manageable, but it actually enables you to see progress really is being made, one small task at a time.

Making progress and improvements everyday is so important, even if it's just a 1 per cent improvement from the previous day. Making small, incremental, but consistent improvements is a much more effective approach to achieving your goals than binge working - a burst of activity then a long break.

> **"DON'T TRY TO TACKLE THE BIG GOAL, BREAK EVERYTHING DOWN INTO TASKS AND MILESTONES AND WORK ON THEM CONSISTENTLY."**

The best way to achieve this is to sit down and plan, either with others or by yourself. Get a big pad or piece of paper and write down your ultimate end goal, that big dream or idea. You need to reverse engineer it and work backwards. Underneath your big dream, write down up to 10 tasks that you need to achieve in order to reach that goal. Rank each of those 10 things in order of priority and importance. Then under each of those 10 things, split them up into 10 more tasks. By now you might have up to 100 tasks that you need to achieve to reach that end goal.

Of course, depending on how big your goal is you might need to split those last 10 tasks down even further. You might be able to control some of those tasks completely and put a timescale on them. Other tasks might be more vague or they may depend on external factors, such as other people. But whatever your dream or vision is, the more you break it down, the more control you will have and the more progress you will make towards achieving your goal. You might even want to break it down to the point where each micro task is 30 minutes to an hour of work. Breaking it down to this level really makes you see how achievable that big goal is, because you can see all the steps you need to take to get there. Over time, as you and your business evolve, those steps might change slightly, but having this broken down plan in place gives you more confidence in achieving your goal.

Having everything broken down like this is also much easier on your family life. It enables you to see each and every minor task you need to undertake to get closer to that big goal.

Because you have micro tasks that may only take 30 minutes to an hour, you can fit these into times when the kids are asleep, or any downtime such as during travel on a bus or train, or even just an hour before everyone wakes up. Having these micro tasks lined up means you can fit them easily into busy family life.

QUICK STORY

At the time of writing this book, I'm involved in operating and running a technology and consulting business as well as property development. I'm also hosting and producing my own podcast and making sure I'm able to juggle being a dad at the same time. There is always a lot going on but I manage it all, simply by breaking it all down into a micro schedule.

Within each of my businesses and projects, I started at the very top with that big end goal in mind. I might have a specific time frame to achieve that goal. I then break it down into goals I need to achieve each year, and then I split up the goals into monthly milestones, and from there I can then create tasks that need to be completed to achieve those goals. I break it down further into micro tasks that can be achieved within 1 hour, 30 minute and 15 minute activities. This way I can see the exact actions I need to take to build towards that big goal. I will always have that big goal at the back of my mind, but it's not what I'm focused on throughout the days, weeks and months.

When you think about it, most tasks can be achieved within an hour. If it can't, it should be broken down further so you can easily manage progress on that task. It also feels great as you tick off each micro task. I can usually accomplish many of the 30 and 15 minute tasks around the kids, particularly if I can work on them passively. They say that multitasking is actually counterproductive, in that when you focus on too many tasks at the same time, you don't end up getting much done. This is only true if those tasks both require you to be fully active. I often layer up my tasks so I'm working on an active task whilst working on another passively. Quite often I will be bathing the kids or changing nappies whilst on the phone briefing or having a conference call with my team, speaking to suppliers or partners. By layering those passive micro 30 or 15 minute tasks on top of activities that do require you to be active, you can achieve a lot more in a short space of time. In fact, as I've written this chapter of the book (my 1 hour active micro task), I am sitting in the car waiting for my daughter, who's at her school friend's birthday party. During this time I've also been able to complete three of my under 30 minute tasks passively whilst writing this chapter. I've been on the phone to two potential investors for projects within our property development business, and I've also used the text-to-speech function on my smartphone to read out the weekly written report my team produced for me. This feature essentially reads out the highlighted words on a document, saving the time it takes to physically read it. Within the space of an hour and a half, I have managed to tick four micro tasks off my list that perhaps would have taken me double the time had I not layered them passively.

Break down your goals into micro tasks and layer passive tasks on top of active tasks. Try to make your active tasks into passive ones where possible so you can achieve more at the same time. For example, I often use a dictation and voice recognition app, which means I can now write that email by voice whilst in the car, instead of having to actively sit at my computer or device.

Be flexible

In real business life, the original plan will rarely stay the same. You need to be prepared to be flexible and ready to make changes as your business evolves and the situation changes. Your goal doesn't change, but the tasks within the plan will become more refined, as you come up with better ideas, get better at what you do and become more efficient.

I've followed this basic model in each of my businesses, and I refine it with each new idea. My goals are more complex now, and tasks are broken down at least ten levels deep. I have different teams to help me achieve each of those tasks, but the model of thinking and planning remains the same.

Section Two

STARTING YOUR BUSINESS

9

TAKE THAT LEAP OF FAITH AND START YOUR BUSINESS

Just like having a child and becoming a parent, there's no perfect time to start a business. There are more beneficial times than others, but there will never be a perfect time. There will always be better situations - the economy could always be better, your product or service could always be more refined and you could always have more money to fall back on.

While there may not be a *perfect* time, there are three things you *do* need to be certain of:

- **Having financial backup** If your business doesn't bring in revenue straight away or things don't quite go to plan, how are you going to feed your family and pay the bills?
- **Having a market for your business** Have you proven that there is definitely demand for your product or service?

- **Having a plan for balancing your time** How are you going to balance your role as a parent and businessperson?

What is your financial backup plan?

Starting a business is very exhilarating – as you're planning it, your mind starts to wonder about all the benefits, money and freedom you're going to gain from your new venture. But during these times of excitement and planning for the good times, you also have to plan for the bad times. Alongside your plan for success, you also need a contingency plan. What if something beyond your control happens in the market or the economy and it sets you back? You need to ensure this won't affect your family.

While you're planning your business, you need to ensure that your basic family expenses are covered. Rent or mortgage payments, food, education, childcare costs and bills must all be covered at the bare minimum. You may have savings that will last a certain period of time, but if you don't you should try to make sure you have some fallback money before you consider making the leap.

While planning your success, you may not want to think about these things, but having these areas covered will also free up your mind to focus on building your business without having to worry about how you'll cover basic household costs if things don't go as well as you hoped. Having this as part of your plan means you're fully covered and have peace of mind.

Is there a definite demand for your business?

Perhaps your business idea will fill a gap in an industry that you already work in, or provide a better service or product. In this case you already know there is a market for it, you just need to reach that audience.

On the other hand, your product or service could be totally new. I've been involved in, and seen, many business start-ups where the product or service is so new and innovative that there isn't already a proven market there. It could be a new product or service that solves a problem that no other product currently solves. You need to ensure that you have done enough market research, or at least know your intended customers will actually want or need your product or service.

Starting a business in a brand new category without the market research to back you up is risky. While you may feel your product or service provides the perfect solution to a particular problem, or fills a gap in the market, others may perceive your idea differently. Getting feedback directly from potential customers is a must in this situation.

Write down a brief plan for how to get feedback from your target market. It's a good idea to create an audience persona – a fictional character based on your target audience's real characteristics. You could start with something basic like this list:

- Give them a name for this exercise, so you can refer to them during your planning.
- Are they male, female or is gender not a factor?
- What age bracket?
- What is their income bracket?
- Are they single, coupled up, married, parents?
- What is their profession? You can be as general or specific as you want, e.g. office based, works at big marketing agency or even as specific as 'graphic designer'.
- What kind of products and services do they buy that are similar to yours?

Now you need to find your target audience to get feedback on your product or service. Take a look at your existing circle – if you have family or friends that fit your target audience, this is the best place to start. Outside that circle you can find people online, perhaps in forums, social networking groups or even physical networking groups. Ask your target audience how they feel about the problem you're hoping to solve – it may be a smaller or bigger problem than you anticipated. Ask them how they feel about your product or service and how you intend to present it to the end user. Don't forget to ask them about price. Finally, ask them if they would buy your product if you launched it.

All of this feedback will still only be an indicator, but once you've gathered enough data you'll start to see how strong the demand could be for your product. Depending on what sector your business is in you might need to get feedback from hundreds of individuals (or fewer if the market is niche). For example, if your business idea is a high price item and is aimed at large businesses, you only really need feedback from a few targets. But if you are a Business to Consumer (B2C) business, and you're hoping to sell your product to the masses, you obviously need feedback from a lot more people.

How to balance your time between family and business

It's great starting a business, but once you've started it you've got to run it – operating a business is far more difficult than just starting one. When you have a family to raise as well, you need to make sure you're getting the balance right. It's so easy to get carried away with your new venture and work on it every hour of the day. You have to try to draw a line and ring-fence some time each day to focus on the family, regardless of what's happening in your business. This is not just important for your family, but for your own wellbeing too.

QUICK STORY

Before having children, I worked every day of the week and every hour that I could. My poor wife hardly ever saw me, but over time, as the business started to become more stable, I could reserve certain hours for my wife.

When our first child Natasha arrived, I knew that I couldn't work every single hour of the day. I mellowed and realised that a happy life is about balance. I would reserve one day of the weekend where I wouldn't even think about work, not even check my work emails or systems. The other day of the weekend, I would only look over things when everyone was asleep, but during the waking hours of the weekend I was all theirs. I found this to have two benefits - it actually gives you an excuse for some time out and to rest your brain. You can't physically focus on work seven days a week over a long period of time and not burn out. During the week I would fully focus on running my business, but during the weekend I would need to wind down and recharge.

Everyone's schedule and routine will be different, and you may find that during the week you need to take some time out for family duties, but get some work in during the weekend. The important thing here is recognising early on, that running a business requires a lot of hard work, but it also requires you to be physically and mentally healthy. At the end of the day you have to think about why you are building your business in the first place.

Build your business, but also make time for your family. It is possible to do both well with the right balance.

10

BUILD SYSTEMS, PROCESSES AND ANCHORS

Becoming a parent entrepreneur is always going to be tough. Building a business and raising a family at the same time – there's a whole lot of craziness and chaos in both endeavours. Even just being a parent means there are times when you don't know whether you're coming or going. The screaming, crying and tantrums can almost be too much. The weeks go by incredibly quickly and the 'crazy' doesn't ever seem to simmer down. If parenting alone wasn't hectic enough, throw starting a business into the mix and it might just tip you over the edge.

If you're to survive and excel as a parent in business, you need to set up systems, processes and anchors to help you keep control, build momentum and succeed. Having these in place can give you another level of assurance and stability when challenging situations arise out of the blue. As most parents will know, it's common for a child to fall ill and you have to drop everything to attend to them. Knowing that you have these systems, anchors and processes in place means you can avoid the stress, making you a calmer parent and business owner.

Anchors

As a parent entrepreneur, life is going to be crazy, chaotic and mind-blowingly stressful at times. To keep it together you need to be able to regulate and channel the rollercoaster of emotions, and control the situation in your head, even amid the chaos.

> **ANCHORS STABILISE ALL THE CHAOS THAT'S GOING ON IN YOUR LIFE, AND HELP YOU BUILD MOMENTUM.**

Anchors are activities that you do no matter what happens, whether the day has been a roaring success or an absolute disaster, and no matter how you feel emotionally. The anchors are designed to bring you stability, at least in your mind, and to neutralise any bad or negative thoughts that have managed to creep in.

Choose two or three activities you can do each week, no matter what happens. You can choose more, but because the anchors are a must-do, be realistic about what you can fit in. If you miss any anchors, this safety net doesn't work and you can end up feeling even worse.

QUICK STORY

I chose two very simple anchors. I go to the gym at least once per week and have a movie or games night with a bottle of wine (for me) with the kids, every Saturday, no matter what happens and no matter where I am. You might have just read that and thought, well that's pretty easy – it's meant to be. Anchors aren't supposed to be difficult, the purpose is not to stress yourself, but to set an activity that you can do consistently, no matter what else happens. Over time, this brings about an easy routine that will naturally spread to other areas of your life – and so will the feeling of stability that comes with it.

My two anchors give me exercise and relaxation, both physically and mentally. I haven't overstretched myself and I know that week in, week out, I can achieve and hit these anchors, which give me the feeling of calm, routine and consistency. They help me focus mentally and bring me back down to earth when things are going really well, but also get me back up on my feet when I'm feeling stressed.

Here's how to choose your anchors:

- **Choose anchors you enjoy** If you don't enjoy them they won't last, then they're pointless. Make sure you choose something you'll look forward to.
- **Choose an anchor that has some kind of added value** I chose the gym because I'm constantly rushing and often don't eat as well as I should, so I want to burn off all the fast and convenience foods that I consume whilst on the road. The goal is simply to feel a little bit fitter and healthier.
- **Choose an anchor that makes you feel relaxed** After all the stress and hard work involved in being a parent entrepreneur, it's worth having an anchor that relaxes you. For me, the movie or games night with a bottle of wine combines one-to-one time with my kids with wind-down time. It also gives my wife a night off.
- **Choose an anchor that you can do anywhere** If you're on holiday or away from your normal routine for any period of time, you don't want to miss your anchors. Choose an activity that you can either do wherever you are or at least access remotely.

Systems

Create a system for storing your work, thoughts and ideas. This doesn't need to be complicated – choose something that fits you and your lifestyle and not the other way round. For some it might literally just be a pen and pad. Richard Branson carries a notepad everywhere he goes. He often says 'An idea not written down is an idea lost. When inspiration calls, you've got to capture it.'

Most people carry around a smartphone, and there are a plethora of productivity apps to help you organise your life. I use two very simple apps on my phone that not only allow me to make a note of any ideas that hit me wherever I am, but also help me run my business.

QUICK STORY

I use the simple built-in Notes app on my phone, which stores all of my notes in the cloud. This allows me to access them on any of my other devices. In fact, this entire book was written on the notes app before transferring it to a more publishable format.

Having my notes for this book stored in the cloud allowed me to work on it wherever I was. I could add or tweak sections between meetings or even while having lunch. I also use the Notes app to jot down all my ideas, compose long emails or project briefs as a starting point, before transferring to other channels, platforms or software.

I also use several project management apps. They are cloud-based and allow me to create boards to manage a particular project, or even an entire organisation. You can have as many different boards as you like. Within the boards are cards for individual tasks - think of them as sticky notes - but with the power to be able to upload attachments, add notes and include deadlines. The best thing is the ability to collaborate with others, and allocate boards and cards to people in your team. Using these cloud applications allows me to monitor the progress of tasks and projects, and allows for fast, documented communication between members of my team. I even use these tools to manage our family life, holidays, home improvement projects and kids' outings.

Choose systems, apps and software that will help you become more efficient. Here's how to choose a good system:

- **Choose systems that are easy for you to understand and master** Don't choose something for the fancy interface – if it doesn't work it's going to hinder you, not help you. Choose something that does the job and if it happens to be a simple pen and notebook, then use that.
- **Choose systems that you can access anywhere** Nowadays, almost everything is online and in the cloud. Choose an app or software you can access wherever you are in the world and on any device. If your device gets lost or broken, you need to be able to access your work on another device without too much trouble.
- **Choose a system that you can share and collaborate on with others if needed** You don't want to do any exporting, or copy and pasting, and you certainly don't want to duplicate files to send an email. Where possible, you need one master copy of your notes and documents that you can share with others if you need to, so that any new changes are reflected

on that master version. The danger of sharing files via email is that you may start to lose track of who has the latest version.

Processes and habits

As with your systems, you need to design a way of doing things, an order in which things need to happen, and form some kind of habit or consistency. Processes don't have to be ultra technical, they just form a routine for what you do on a daily, weekly and monthly basis. If you have young kids you'll already know the power of routine. The bedtime routine, the morning routine or the school run routine are the obvious ones.

These processes or routines might not be something you can just think of and do, they may be something you develop over time as you start your business. Many of these routines might not directly serve a purpose or add direct value, but may help re-programme your mind and drive momentum that will help you in other areas of your life.

Some years ago I saw a news item where a Navy Seal Commander talked about the importance of making your bed in the morning. He explained how this routine task can have a positive impact on your wellbeing and behaviour throughout the rest of the day. Essentially, making your bed sets the tone for the day – if you start the day productively and on the right foot, the rest of the day will follow suit.

> **WHATEVER MAKES YOU FEEL PRODUCTIVE IS WHAT YOU SHOULD DO TO START THE DAY OR WEEK.**

It might be exercise, it might be having a coffee whilst reading the newspaper, or it might be doing something with the kids. Whatever it is, you should set it as a habit. This in turn fuels routine and consistency, and that feeling will naturally transfer to the rest of your activities throughout the day. When done over time, this can have a hugely positive effect in your family and business life.

QUICK STORY

Over the years I've developed some quite strange habits both at home and at work that help me get myself and my mind in order. They serve no direct purpose to my business, or to me as a parent, but help me form a consistent, mental routine

I have several money tree plants throughout our house, and I water them all every Sunday without fail. If I'm on holiday I have to get someone else to water them, but it has to be done on a Sunday. Doing this every Sunday helps me set the tone for Monday. It's a strange ritual but I've been doing it for years, and like my anchors, it helps me form consistency in other areas of my life.

In my business, I like to start my working day on the phone. I try to make the most of my calls in the morning, whether that's to clients, investors, business partners or my staff. Making those calls kick starts momentum for the day, and makes me feel I've begun the day productively.

11

CREATE HABIT-FORMING PRODUCTS AND SERVICES

Getting new customers is difficult and requires a lot of groundwork, both in marketing and in the actual sales process. This can be very labour-intensive. You need repeat custom and a product or service that customers will keep coming back for.

> **"WHATEVER PRODUCT OR SERVICE YOU'RE SELLING, MAKE SURE THERE'S LONGEVITY IN IT."**

Think of the printer business model. Printers used to be very cheap to buy – there was a point when printer manufacturers were practically giving them away. This was because they didn't make money on the printers, they made it on the printer ink or toner. Back then, printers were designed so you could only use the ink cartridges that the printer manufacturer produced, so once you started using their printers you were almost always tied into buying their ink or toner too. Nowadays, third party ink and toner cartridge companies have found a way to bypass this, so you have much more choice and aren't forced to buy directly from the printer manufacturer. As a business model, it was brilliant. Think about how you can adapt your business so that people will keep coming back to you.

When I started my first business, I sold a service that was project based. This one-time service helped people set up their website and online marketing presence. One thing I quickly realised was that once I had finished a project, I had to keep finding new customers to continue making money. No matter what product or service you are offering, you need to find a way to encourage customers to keep buying from you time and time again.

One way to build longevity into your business is to be at the forefront of your customers' minds, whether they need the product at the time or not. The UK sofa company DFS is a good example of this. DFS constantly has a sale and advertises heavily on television, radio and in print. You only buy a sofa once every few years, but when you do need one, you always remember DFS because they are constantly reminding you they have a sale on – *they always do.*

QUICK STORY

Over the years, I've used various methods to be constantly on my customer's radar so that whenever they need a solution, my products and services are there at the forefront of their minds. For low-spend clients, we keep them informed of what's happening in the industry, what's new and what they need to keep an eye out for. We send them a monthly email with a summary and breakdown of everything that's happening in the industry. There's no sales message, no pushy call to actions – just a simple update on industry news and a reminder that we're here when they need us.

For high-spend clients, with whom we have a much more integrated relationship, I personally call for a catch-up and a chat. Not necessarily about work, sometimes just to chew the fat about family, what competitors are doing and generally about what's going on. This is similar to the monthly newsletter but on a much more personal level. This constant catch-up builds strong relationships. When the client needs you they know you are accessible to them - you become an extension of their team.

I also make sure investors get a personalised catch-up. It's not always about deals or business, it's usually just a general conversation about everything happening in the industry and what we're working on with other clients or investors.

Over the years, some of those general conversations have turned into lucrative business deals and projects. Had we not kept in touch, perhaps some of those deals would have gone to a competitor or never happened at all.

Some of the brokers who deal with me on the property business do something similar. I can always tell that they are calling for a catch-up, to see what I've been up to in property and to remind me that they are around if I need any help from them.

If you are at the beginning of your business, remember to schedule catch-ups and updates with clients or customers and investors. Sometimes these ordinary catch-ups can form the cornerstone of your business and turn into lucrative, business-changing deals.

12

MASTERING THE ART OF DELEGATION AND FOCUS

When you're starting a business and raising family at the same time, to remain in control of both these areas of your life, you need to constantly evaluate when to focus and when to delegate. You simply can't do everything, that's a fact. You need to ensure you're only focusing on the top priorities, and the rest you need to delegate to someone else, or put on the back burner. Figure out what needs your attention and your attention only, as in no one else can perform that particular task, and focus only on those things.

In our household, my wife is the boss. She runs our family and makes the daily decisions for the kids. It's not a conscious decision and we've never had a formal conversation about it – it just happened. Things such as what the kids eat, what they wear, our family diary, school activities and weekend activities – these are just a few examples of the many decisions that my wife is in charge of on a daily basis. My main focus is to build for our future financially, produce income and make sure my family has a comfortable life. I also get heavily involved in the daily operations of the family, like helping with homework, dinner times, bath times and bedtimes, but the decisions are made by my wife. She runs the show at home and I am delegated my share of the household chores. We also share other family decisions like moving house, education and schooling, or where we want to go on holidays.

When you're starting and running a business, there are already so many major and minor, short-term and long-term decisions to make that you can't dilute that focus by spreading yourself too thinly. You need to know which tasks and decisions you should delegate and then figure out who to delegate them to. Whilst you might be able to delegate decisions and tasks at home to your partner or other family members, in business it's not quite so simple. Decisions, even minor ones, can make or break your business. At first you might not be able to take on full-time staff, but there are still bound to be things that you can delegate.

QUICK STORY

When I started my first business as a marketing freelancer I had to wear every hat there was: designer, marketer, accountant and book-keeper, sales person, admin person, and even HR in some cases. Wearing several hats is common in business and that's what you need to do when you start out, but there will be some tasks that aren't so important.

I was so busy that I wasn't able to answer calls from what could have been potential clients. I was missing out on new business opportunities. To solve this problem, I hired a virtual PA answering service. My calls were routed through to the service and they would answer in my business name. They had a script, and if they couldn't answer a question the caller had, they would take a message and pass it onto me. I could then call back in-between tasks. As well as ensuring I wasn't missing any important calls, it also gave the customer a professional impression that I had someone answering my calls. This is quite common practice in today's fast-paced business world.

It was because I had the virtual PA service that I was able to catch one particular client who called whilst I was in a meeting. That same client is still a client today, under a different service offering, and has grown to become one of my biggest. Had it not been for the answering service, that client may have tried someone else and we would have never met.

There are many ways to decide which tasks and decisions to focus on and where to delegate. I usually ask myself three questions when looking at my list of tasks:

Does this task or decision carry any measurable value? It might be obvious, but quite often you find yourself doing so many things, you don't have time to weigh up how much value a particular task actually carries. Quite often you'll find that certain tasks don't even need to be done because they don't carry any measurable value straight away. These tasks can either be put on the back burner or delegated.

Will it make money now? When you're starting a new business, or in the early years, every single decision needs bring in revenue, especially if you are bootstrapping (I cover this in chapter 7). When you're reviewing your huge lists of tasks, look at what can bring you the quickest revenue and put those tasks right at the top of the list. Nothing is more important than bringing in revenue, because without cash flow, your business is not going to grow very quickly, nor will it survive for very long. Forget the fancy logo or designs if there are tasks that can bring money in now. Delegate anything that doesn't positively impact your cash flow.

Will it help me grow my business in the long-term? Of course there are going to be some tasks which might not bring you revenue straight away, but will help you grow your business in the long-term. These tasks are important too, but not as important as making sure your business survives. If you need to work on tasks that bring in income now, as well as long-term value-adding tasks that will help you grow in the future, you can use the 80/20 rule. Spend 80 per cent of your time on tasks that generate revenue for today and 20 per cent of your time on creating future value.

As your business grows you can bring in staff to help you. Then you can start to offload some of these decisions to them at a micro level and you can concentrate on some of the higher-level decisions.

QUICK STORY

In the early years of running a digital marketing agency with my former business partner, there were just two of us doing everything. When we were able to bring in staff, we chose someone who was able to help us look after the daily operations, which then freed me from the day-to-day tasks. Instead, I was able to focus on higher-level tasks such as working on client pitches and helping to market our services to new clients. As we grew even more, we hired more people to help look after specific parts of the business operations, leaving my business partner and I to look for and go after even bigger clients. It was because we were able to delegate those small day-to-day tasks that we could grow relatively quickly.

Focus on the tasks that make money now and help you grow in the future. Delegate the rest.

13

WHY PERFECTION WILL KILL YOUR BUSINESS FAST

When I was a young boy, my dad taught me an old saying, 'Ride a cow to find a horse'. What it means is, don't just wait around for a horse. If you have to ride a cow to find the horse, then so be it (in others words, don't wait for perfection, just do what it takes to get something done).

Today, most new start-up businesses don't survive their first year. Businesses, particularly new start-ups, are all about speed. The quicker you are at going to market and getting those sales in, the higher the chance of success.

Many people start a business with a vision of their product or service and set about trying to build the perfect version of their vision. There's nothing wrong with wanting to build a great product or service – who doesn't want to offer their potential customers the very best? But there's got to be a balance between getting something to market and taking a long time to refine your service or product.

Is what you're selling good enough?

This is where a Minimal Viable Product (MVP) comes into play. An MVP is a version of your product or service that is developed to an acceptable quality. It's not quite the full perfect product that you had in your vision, but the point is to develop something quickly that's good enough to sell and continually refine.

You might have done plenty of market research around your product or service, its demand, the price points your market is willing to pay and even how you will deliver it. In reality, market research only goes so far to prove that you have a real business proposition. The best type of market research is to get something real and working out there into the market to see if it sells and to see what customers think about it. The truth is, your market research may tell you that people demand a certain product, but there are many external factors that could affect people's opinions of your product or service, even if you have followed all the feedback from the research.

External factors that could affect your product or service include market changes, how you market your product and even legal changes, to name but a few. The world today moves so quickly that your market and industry could literally change whilst you are building your perfect product or service. By the time you're ready to release it, the market may have moved on and your product or service could already be out of date. This is particularly true in technology-based businesses, or where technology plays a big role in that industry as a disruptor.

QUICK STORY

A friend who has two young children wanted to start a side business that she could run around her family life. She was really passionate about baking and saw it as an opportunity to create celebration cakes for birthdays, weddings and other events. She was used to baking for her family but wasn't sure if it was good enough to sell, so she decided to test the market. She made a customised birthday cake for a friend's birthday - the cake was designed to look like a campervan that resembled the one her friend had. Every detail was perfect, even down to the bumps and scratches on the actual campervan. At the birthday, her cake got a lot of attention and feedback on the unique customised design. She set up a Facebook page and as word spread, she started to get orders in from people she didn't even know. She was able to start the business purely from testing out her product on people that are likely to buy, and she's able to do this around the school run and family life.

Marketing

How you market your product could also affect the way your product performs, regardless of the results of your market research. Marketing is extremely important when it comes to launching your product. How people perceive your product or service could be the difference between an overnight success or a gradual flop. Just because the market research indicated your product would sell, doesn't mean those same people questioned would actually buy your product. The way they are marketed to makes a big difference to how they respond to your product or your service. New businesses often fail to recognise the importance of branding and marketing because they are not perceived to be direct sales channels, but they contribute the most to how your product is perceived and if it will ultimately sell.

The importance of speed

Mark Zuckerberg, CEO of Facebook, once said: 'Move fast and break things', which essentially means build something and keep improving it. Getting your product to market quickly means you can test if it's going to sell as well as you want it to in the real world, and if not, what tweaks you need to make to get it to sell.

The best way to build your MVP is to list every single feature of your product or service, putting each item under the headings of short, medium and long-term features.

The short-term list will contain the most essential features for your product or service to work. It might mean selling this pared-down version at a lower price than your final product, but the aim of this MVP is to test out the market and see if there is an appetite for what you're doing. You may find that your product sells but you then encounter problems delivering to or servicing customers, because you hadn't properly thought out some of the processes after you sold it. The feedback from your MVP can be added to your next list.

Under medium-term, take the feedback from the people who bought your MVP and use it to improve your product or service. Here you can also start adding some of the wish-list features you had in your original vision. At this stage you're making your product better and more sophisticated. You're discovering new ways to deliver your product or service to the customer, but you are continually collecting feedback to improve your product too.

In your long-term list, you are going to get your product to the point where it is almost perfect. By now you have ironed out all the problems from two levels of real-world feedback. The product or service should be pretty slick now and you will have processes in place to deliver it.

Your product or service should now be at a stage where it can be scaled up. It's a great position to be in where you have a polished product to sell to the masses.

14

WORK ANYWHERE AND EVERYWHERE

When you're starting a business, you want your overheads to be as low as possible. Your workspace is usually the highest of the overheads, so if you can get the cost of this right down you'll have a great head start. It's a good idea to try to prolong the period where you don't need to rent a place for work for as long as possible. Depending on the type of business you are starting, you may not even need to rent a workplace.

If you need a street presence, such as a retail shop, food or drink outlet, you may not want to commit to a long-term lease. You might want to test out the market by operating from a temporary stall, or set up as a pop-up shop, to have a street presence relatively quickly without the long-term commitments of a permanent retail unit.

Working from home

If your business is office-based, that makes things even more flexible. Try working from home for as long as possible. If you have people working for you, and you have space at home, you may be able to turn an area into a makeshift office until you have the stream of revenue to sustain the ongoing rent of office premises.

Technology makes it possible to work almost anywhere nowadays, as long as you set everything up in the cloud and all you need is an internet connection.

The most ideal solution is a spare room in the house, such as a conservatory, an attic or a garage, that you can convert into a home office. If not, you could convert a garden shed into an office. I've seen some sheds converted into some pretty funky home offices! If you don't have a dedicated spare room, you could even just screen off a section of another room, like a desk behind the dining room, which can be stored away when you're not working. Any warm place with an internet connection and electricity will fit the bill.

Although being able to work from home might seem like a dream come true to some, when you're a parent with kids, especially young kids, the logistics of working from home become a little more complicated. Most parents of young kids will know that no matter where you hide, the little ones will always find you and they will always want to be where they're not supposed to be. It's also important to set work and home boundaries, communicate to your family that although you are physically there, that when you are at your desk it's time for you to work.

QUICK STORY

In the very early days of my business career, we lived in a small two bedroom house and we didn't have any spare room for me to set up a dedicated office. Instead I found some space under the stairs where I could squeeze in a small desk and chair. It was in the living room, so even though I was under the stairs I could still be visible. I installed a curtain I could draw on, and would hide the space under the stairs. With a pair of headphones and the curtains drawn it was like I was in my own dedicated space, and for a couple of years I managed to build the business from that small but functional space.

Making the most of the cloud

Over the years I have transitioned my businesses into cloud-based enterprises, where all the vital information and processes for me to run and operate my business are in the cloud. I have staff, partners and investors located across multiple cities and countries, but as long as I have one of my devices with me, such as a laptop, iPad or phone, I can operate my business. This gives me the freedom to be able to work from just about anywhere – a great bonus when family time is at a premium.

Of course there are times I have to go to the office for staff meetings, or go to see clients, partners or investors face to face, but generally I can operate 90 per cent of my business directly from the cloud. I believe that more and more businesses will be able to operate fully in the cloud as technology and connection speeds evolve.

QUICK STORY

So how do I manage staff remotely? Over the years I had assembled a team that I could trust and depend on to support me and I was at the front of the business - I was the face and clients bought me. Most of my clients were in the UK but some were based in the USA and Europe. My team was spread out and I had developed a way we could work across different time zones with ease. I developed contracts and processes with my team where work did not depend on a 9 to 5 basis. I couldn't control the 9 to 5 because I was always out with clients and I didn't like the thought of tying people down for certain periods of time just because it was office hours. So I developed a cloud-based working environment in which we could control all projects, and all communications, including those with clients (Read more about systems, process and anchors in chapter 10).

All I asked for were some core hours when everyone must be available, but other than that, I didn't care when or where they worked, as long as targets were hit and deadlines were met. I didn't care if my team worked less during the day and more at night if that suited them. This flexible approach to the working day is one that really suits people with families. One of my key members of the team had become a new dad and his wife was unwell. Although I didn't ask him to, he was able to work from the hospital and the whole thing was seamless.

Using a cloud-based system works well with the types of businesses I run. I can see at any one time exactly what everyone is doing and where we are up to with projects, and the team can see what I'm doing - if I'm in meetings and when I'm available if they need me. As long as projects are delivered on time, timescales are kept on track and the team is always available at certain core times, that works for me. It also works for them because it means they don't need to take time off for doctor's appointments or school runs.

Co-working spaces

Technology now allows you to work anytime and anywhere, and to use any dead time that you have to be productive. If working from home isn't viable for you because the chaos of having kids makes it too difficult to concentrate, and renting an office is out of your budget, the emergence of co-working spaces is the perfect remedy. A co-working space is essentially a big open plan office, divided into hot desks for people to come and go as they please. It's the perfect place to start a business, especially if you're a freelancer. It's a great way to have a place to work without the high rents of a dedicated office. Co-working also allows you to meet like-minded business owners just starting out, and can form the basis of a great support network. For people who feel that working alone at home might be too isolating, co-working can provide a great solution.

> **YOU CAN LITERALLY WORK ANYWHERE AND EVERYWHERE.**

What I've learnt over the years is that running a business no longer means you have to be tied down to a specific location, nor to specific hours of the day, all the time.

15

LOOK BUSY BEFORE YOU ACTUALLY GET BUSY

Imagine you're walking down a street looking for a restaurant to eat at. The street is filled with different types of restaurant - you see some empty ones and some that are packed full of people. Which one do you choose? Naturally, most people would lean towards the restaurant that is full of diners all enjoying their meals. The food must be good, because everyone seems to be eating there. That's how business works. You don't *get* busy until you *look* busy. Customers are less likely to buy from you if others haven't. No one wants to be first. How else do they know if you're any good?

Show the customer what you can do

If you are just starting out, or it's early on in your business journey and customers or clients aren't quite flooding through the doors, you have to make yourself appear busy. Give away freebies or do something for free that demonstrates how good your product or service is.

QUICK STORY

When I started my first freelance marketing business, I only had a handful of small clients. To get more in the beginning I had to do some projects for free to get experience under my belt, demonstrate what value I could bring to their business and to build a reputation. I also took on some pro bono work, which is essentially free work. I naturally became confident in my skills and as I built my portfolio, new clients would hear about me and became clients themselves. Even the people who I did the pro bono work for became clients. It wasn't long before I built a good reputation and got a steady stream of projects.

To this very day, even though I've had several businesses under my belt and several years of experience, I still apply the same model. In the consultancy business, we always start with adding value upfront before we even get the client. We do this especially for the larger clients - we invest a significant amount of time and work into getting the client to choose us. We know that a lot of competitors aren't prepared to give away precious time, particularly at this level where day rates can be quite significant for an entire team to work on a client for free.

> But adding value upfront and giving away your time and work to the client, shows them what it's like to work with you and how committed you are. It doesn't matter if the client is worth £100 or £100,000, we always give added value upfront to give them a taste of what we can do for them.

If your business is retail based, give away samples of your products. If you are in hospitality, launch a free event and invite local people, or better still invite influencers who might just help you spread the word. If you are a service-based business, offer to do a small project or task for free if you can use your potential client as a case study.

A little bit of investment upfront will do wonders in kick-starting any kind of business.

Get help from your family and friends

Sometimes, even though you are willing to give away your products or services for free in exchange for experience or reviews, it can be difficult to find so-called guinea pigs. In the early years you could turn to family and friends for help and support, they are more likely to want to help you than strangers will. Make it fun for them and get them involved in the business. This early support can also help you build a loyal fan base as they start telling their friends and family - a recommendation from a mutual friend is far more powerful than from a stranger.

QUICK STORY

When I was a young kid, my parents started a restaurant business and they found themselves competing against busier, more established restaurants in the area.

They invited close friends, local neighbours, and nearby fellow business owners for the opening week, and seated them all at tables near the window where they could easily be seen from the outside. From the street it looked like a bustling restaurant, so anyone passing would be intrigued about this new place to eat. This tactic created a 'buzz' and worked well. They got me involved and I helped distribute leaflets and menus throughout the local neighbourhood, and I would ask my friends to pass them onto their parents. Before long the restaurant became genuinely busy. As people talked about the restaurant to their friends and family, it built up a good reputation, and my parents established a steady flow of regular customers. They built that restaurant from the ground up for ten years before they retired. I worked in the restaurant myself, and as I watched my parents operate their successful business, it helped me develop my own skills that I still utilise today.

16

DON'T NEGLECT YOUR PARTNER

Starting a new business means working on your new venture during free hours every day. Having young kids can already take its toll on your relationship with your partner. Then, factor in that you will have even less time with them and more time working on your business and that can really put a strain on a relationship. It's really important that your partner understands your goals and what you are working towards. If your visions for your life together are aligned, it can actually make your relationship even stronger in the long run.

Your partner isn't necessarily just your wife, husband or significant other. It can be the other person or people in your life that help you raise your children, including your own parents, relatives or friends. When starting up a new business, it's important that all the people in your support network understand what you're doing.

In the beginning, you may think you can take on everything, but at some point you will be met with challenges and stressful times, even if you have your partner onboard. Accepting help and support is very natural. Enlisting help from people within your close circle can really help you and you partner balance their own work, your business and family life. Perhaps someone you trust can help look after the kids or do the odd school run to ease your busy schedule.

Keep your partner in the loop

Involving your partner in the planning stages of the business can help them understand how much work is going to be involved. They don't necessarily need to be completely in it and be hands on, but explaining to them what you are doing can help them see what you're going through and allow them to empathise. In a way, this is their journey too because ultimately it involves them stepping up in areas of family life where you might have to step back slightly.

Running a technology business meant that I was constantly connected and tuned in to my business through all my devices (smart phone, tablet or laptop). It also meant that if there was an emergency such as a server going down, I could fix it from any one of those devices. Quite often I would have to just jump up out of my seat during dinner and go to my laptop to login and fix the issue. My wife Yan was used to this and she understood how much I valued family dinner with her and the kids, so if I did have to get up and go there was always an important reason for it.

Establishing that mutual trust and understanding with your partner from the very beginning makes things much easier and less tense in your relationship further down the line.

Just the two of you

Working hard on your business is necessary, but allocating specific pockets of time for different people in your life is not only important, it's also better for your health and well-being. When life is taken up by either family or business, allocating pockets of dedicated time to your partner can be essential.

Yan and I obviously spend time together when we are with the kids, but we try to have at least one date night per month where it's just the two of us. No kids, no work and no business talk. Quite often it might just be having dinner, doing a bit of shopping together or going to the cinema, but the important thing is that it's just the two of us. Those pockets of time together make you remember what it was like before kids and before you started a business, and the journey that you've been on so far. It makes you both realise why you're working so hard to build your family and business, and it makes you realise that it all started with just the two of you.

For better or worse

Whatever situation you're in, whether you're going through highs or lows, never shut off from your partner. It might seem like you're protecting them, but it's important to make them a part of what you're going through. Share your pain and share your joys with them, because they deserve to be a part of whatever you're going through, but don't overburden them with the details, just make them aware of how you are feeling at the time and let them share in that emotion. Whether they are active in your business or not, you're on this journey together.

Starting a new business, juggling kids and keeping a strong relationship with your partner is never going to be plain sailing, but working together, properly communicating and supporting each other throughout this journey can be invaluable and will help you build a strong future, both as a family and in business.

QUICK STORY

One year, early on in my business career, recession hit the UK and I lost a lot of clients. I couldn't fill the gap in sales quick enough. Yan had a 9 to 5 job at the time and we had no kids, but we had just got married and it was terrible timing for our finances to not be in good shape.

As a teenager I always had a side hustle. I learnt to work hard, earn a good income from several sources and never stop. But since starting my own proper business I thought that was enough. It turns out that you can't rely on your main gig, even when it is your own business. The most successful entrepreneurs, investors and businessmen and women in the world say that you should always have multiple streams of income. My own situation proved to be a case in point. Had I continued with the mentality of having side hustles and having more than one income I wouldn't be in this mess.

I wasn't in a good place in life but something inside told me that this low point was also a turning point and would lead to something much bigger and better. This period of time taught me the importance of perspective and resilience. Yan became my rock, she stepped up and paid all the bills. She never once complained about our situation or even asked when things would be better. She just held the fort and trusted that I would get us out of the situation.

That same year, our house was broken into. All of Yan's wedding jewellery had been taken, as well as some cash and most importantly one of the video cameras with the entire day's wedding footage on it. We were absolutely devastated.

A few months later we got even more terrible news. Yan's dad was diagnosed with an aggressive cancer. The doctors only gave him a few weeks to live and we tried to spend as much time as we could with him. Two weeks later he passed away.

We were in a pretty bad place, and as the year drew to a close, things had become so bad that I could barely afford Christmas. It was the lowest point of my life. I felt like I'd failed. Worse still, I felt like I'd let my wife down. But we both persevered and kept each other in high spirits by constantly communicating. As a team we were determined to get our lives back on track and if anything, it made our relationship even stronger.

As the New Year arrived, I said goodbye to that terrible year and I focused on getting the business back on track, recession or no recession. I started working on a new business plan. I doubled up my efforts developing brand new products and services, and this set the tone for my next stage of growth.

17

THE LONELINESS OF RUNNING A BUSINESS

No one tells you when you start a business just how lonely it can be, emotionally speaking. There are many aspects of being a business owner that the people around you will never fully understand. Running a business can be an emotional rollercoaster, especially when you are also dealing with the challenges of raising children too.

Don't overburden family with daily business worries

As a parent, when I first started in business, I always thought that I would share everything with my family - all the ups and all the downs. Whilst it's healthy to share your journey with your family, realistically you can't share everything with them, because there are some things you have to deal with yourself. If you are the breadwinner in your family, or you contribute the most to household income, you'll find that you'll want to shield your family from the really ugly side of business. For example, in the early years, when cash flow can become tight, you don't want your partner or family to have to worry constantly about paying the mortgage or bills. Whilst that might not literally be the case, it's likely that there will be peaks and troughs with cash flow. Of course, there is a distinction between hiding important financial events and knowing what issues are trivial and can be easily solved. All it takes is for a big client to be late in paying their bill for it to start to affect cash flow in the business. Over time, as your business becomes more stable and cash flow becomes more predictable, this is less of a worry, but when you are going through those early years in business, it can become quite stressful.

QUICK STORY

I used to confide in my mum and my wife when things were tough financially in the early years of some of the businesses that I started. What I hadn't realised was that it had a much bigger impact on them than it did on me. Whenever I had any concern about the cash flow in the business, in my mind I would usually have some kind of solution formulating. It might not be a fully developed plan yet, but at least the start of a solution was being plotted in my mind. When I confided and explained these dips in cash flow, which are completely normal in business, to my wife or my mum, they would be overly concerned. Whilst I always told them that I was coming up with a solution, they didn't fully understand that a dip is just a dip. It's not the end of the world, it's just a chalking period in business, which is usually temporary as long as you work hard to fix the problem. Whilst my intention was to share some thoughts from my head and involve family members in my business life, it actually caused some unnecessary concern.

Of course you should share your journey with your family, including the highs and the lows, but don't be so explicit in the lows that it would worry them too much. Don't burden the family too much with the problems and challenges that arc a normal a part of everyday business, especially when you most likely have a solution already formulating in your mind. It's normal for your business to encounter challenges, and this is just part of starting and running a business, but there's no need to over share every detail. However, understanding when it is just a normal dip in business and when there are significant problems, especially ones that will affect family life, is key. Of course, you can't hide those significant problems from them but you can certainly keep those normal dips to yourself to give your family peace of mind. It's time like these that can make the journey in business quite lonely.

Managing your friends' expectations

'But you're the boss now, you can just take a day off if you want…' I lost count of how often friends said this to me when I started in business. In fact, my situation was quite the contrary - they clearly didn't understand that now I was totally accountable for everything. Not only could I not take a day off, but I had to work even harder and even more hours when I could, every day, every week and every month. I literally couldn't afford the time to take holidays, let alone just have a day off when I wanted to. Even if I was ill I had to drag myself into work to make sure that the business continued to operate.

In the early days of business, the reality is that holidays and days off just won't be, and shouldn't even be, in your mind yet. When your friends are working a 9 to 5 job, it can be difficult for them to fully understand what you're going through. It's important to make them understand that everything that goes right or wrong in your business is now down to you, so you can't just go on a random night out because you can't afford to be tired the next day. You have to stay focused. As a parent entrepreneur, you need your friends to appreciate that if you're going to be tired for any reason, it will be because your kids didn't sleep through or they were just a handful, not because you've spent a night on the town. You simply can't afford to lose your focus on the business.

When I first started, I used to tell friends about all the things that were happening on my journey in business. I would share my plans and what my visions for my business were – for me it was exciting, but scary and stressful at the same time. Many of my friends thought success would happen overnight. They became bored of asking about my business when it wasn't making huge strides in progress. The truth is, behind every overnight success we hear about in the press, there are several years of struggle, stress and sacrifice.

One attribute that I learned to master quite quickly is managing FOMO or Fear of Missing Out. As you work on your business, you will no doubt miss out on many social events and it can feel like you're distancing yourself from friends. Sometimes this can make you feel lonely, knowing that whilst your friends might accept you can't see them all the time, they may not fully appreciate and understand what you're actually trying to achieve. Managing this in your mind and reminding yourself of the big picture is important in order to stay focused.

When you're with friends, learn to speak about your business in a more summarised way when asked. Talk less about the intricacies and challenges, and more about the top line things that are happening. I talk more about managing friendships in chapter 20.

Even with staff it's your responsibility

When your business gets to a stage where you start to employ staff, you start to let go of some of the day-to-day operations and delegate some tasks you once did yourself. As they work alongside you to build the business, they may start to understand the main challenges, and whilst they will be more involved in the intricacies of the business than your family and friends, they still won't fully understand the amount of pressure and stress you feel each and every day.

When you're running a business with staff and things go well, you may reward your team but ultimately you stand to benefit the most. When things go wrong, as the business owner you are still 100 per cent accountable for any mistakes made by anyone in the organisation. It could be that you hired the wrong people, don't have the right processes in place to stop mistakes from happening or you just took your eye off the ball. Both the highs and the lows are on your shoulders. The responsibility of this can feel lonely at times.

The loneliness isn't a bad thing

Even the closest people to you may never fully understand what you're going through as a parent business owner. Even with years of running businesses, there are periods where I feel isolated, lonely and unable to fully express the kind of weight that's on my shoulders to those around me. It's difficult for others to fully understand what your vision is and what dreams you're trying to achieve. No one will truly understand what's going through your head, or share the passion you have for your own business.

Whilst no one will completely be able to see and feel your vision for the future, there are networking events and industry gatherings with different themes where like-minded business people gather to share ideas and, on some occasions, have a good night out. These are great for you to not only let your hair down a little, but talk business - something you can't always do with friends. I also belong to a few groups on

Facebook and LinkedIn that are themed around either general business or more specific themes, like technology and property. These can help you share some of what's on your mind and get feedback.

You may not feel the loneliness at first, and if you have business partners or friends in business, you may not feel it for a long time. But even they won't completely understand what your business contributes to your life goals. At some point that loneliness will hit you and you'll suddenly realise that no one in the world fully understands what's going on in your head.

> **EMBRACE THE LONELINESS AND ACCEPT IT AS PART OF BEING A PARENT IN BUSINESS.**

But this loneliness isn't a bad thing. It's actually quite beautiful. It's the one thing only you can see and feel. Only you know where your future's actually heading. While others may not understand, or might even mock your crazy ideas, that's fine because it's not their dream. It's yours.

18

HOW TO JUGGLE BUSINESS AND FAMILY CASH FLOW

If you are just starting out in business, you will have no doubt done a business plan or at least calculated your cash flow, profit and loss. You may or may not have factored in paying yourself anything in your first few years. When I started I certainly didn't, I ploughed everything I had back into the business to try to take it to the next level.

When you have a partner and kids to take care of too, it's not always so easy to go in blindly and plough all your money into your business. As a parent there's always something unexpected to pay for – your kids suddenly grow out of every pair of shoes they have, there's a school trip or there's an unexpected childcare bill to pay.

When you are planning your business on paper, including your profit and loss and cash flow, you need to consider your family's cash flow too. If your partner is also working then that helps, but you should still forecast your business cash flow alongside your family cash flow. Each week and month you should be plotting out all the expected outgoings in your business, as well as any planned family expenditure. It's very easy to say that in your early years in business you will completely cut back. Whilst you or your partner might be able to do this, when you have kids, especially young kids, it's not so easy to make a blanket cut. Factoring in family and child-related expenditure during your business planning is essential so you don't get caught out, or feel like you're depriving your kids of any events or activities.

Live well for less

When planning family events, try to think of every single factor, such as the weather, your friends and extended family or whoever you are with, including specific details such as food, drink and travel. Always look for the cheapest, most cost-effective way to do things.

It is possible to live a socially active family life and to organise activities that are as cost effective as possible. For example, if you have a planned catch-up with friends and the weather is good, instead of going to a theme park, go to the beach, the park or something outdoors which generally doesn't cost as much. Organise picnics instead of eating at restaurants. If the weather is bad, organise things at your house where you can control the budget more, instead of eating out. Even if you can't do this all the time, doing this as often as logistically possible, without compromising on the activity or event itself, can still save you significantly. In the early years of your business it's important to save and budget as often as you can.

Balancing Business and Family Cash Flow

You may already have a system that you follow, but forecasting and planning your cash flow 12 or even 24 months ahead in as much detail as you can, for both your business and family, will take away a lot of stress down the line. Do this in a spreadsheet or cash flow forecast (you can find plenty of templates online). If your budget allows, you should also put in a buffer each month for unexpected costs. This will give you even more control and confidence in your first few years in business.

Most people would have a cash flow forecast in separate spreadsheets - one for business and one for family - but I also have a combined one where I can see all my income and outgoings for both business and family side by side. Most cash flow forecasts are done by calendar month, but a whole month can be a long period when it comes to cash flow. A lot can change within that time period, and in the beginning you want to be as detailed as possible. I did it by day and listed cash by the exact date I knew it was coming in or going out, and if I didn't know I would just put a rough date. Doing it by day takes more management, but you know exactly where you are in terms of cash on a daily basis. When you have your business and family forecast next to each other, you can see the peaks and troughs of overall cash, the time of the month that you might struggle and where either cash in family or business could be temporarily used to help each other's cash position. Remember to list every single outgoing, even if you are not certain if it's an expenditure yet. It's always better to have a buffer.

QUICK STORY

When we had our first child Natasha, I didn't bother with planning. I was at the start of a new business at the time, and as I was already managing cash flow for the business I thought I could do all the forecasting for our family in my head. I had a general idea of the running costs for a young family for nappies, food etc., but even though I had all these rough costs in my head, I found there were many unexpected costs of having a young child. For example, how quickly they grow out of clothes and shoes, or being invited to lots of parent related events and outings. I created my combined daily cash flow forecast, which is slightly different to a normal business cash flow that generally focuses on months. I found that by doing this daily, it gave me a complete overview of where I was overall - family and business. Here's an example:

Business					Family				Total
Date		In	Out	Balance		In	Out	Balance	
				£25,923.00				£8,321.00	
Feb.				£25,923.00				£8,321.00	£ 34,244.00
1st	Client Payment 1	£8,500.00		£34,423.00	Kids Party + Present		-£80.00	£8,241.00	£ 34,244.00
2nd	Utilities		-£273.00	£34,150.00	New Shoes		-£30.00	£8,211.00	£ 42,664.00
3rd	Supplier invoice		-£3,200.00	£30,950.00	Utilities		-£100.00	£8,111.00	£ 42,361.00
4th	Staff		-£6,000.00	£24,950.00	Council Tax		-£110.00	£8,001.00	£ 39,061.00
5th	Travel to meeting		-£50.00	£24,900.00	Mortgage		-£625.00	£7,376.00	£ 32,951.00
6th	Client Payment 2	£3,500.00		£28,400.00	Birthday Party		-£100.00	£7,276.00	£ 32,276.00
7th	New Server		-£500.00	£27,900.00	Rental Property	£625.00		£7,901.00	£ 35,676.00
8th	Accountant		-£300.00	£27,600.00	Supermarket		-£120.00	£7,781.00	£ 35,801.00

It might seem obvious, but having everything itemised down to a daily level like this really empowers you to make decisions quickly.

19

MANAGING SELF-DOUBT AND OVER OPTIMISM

Many people assume that starting a business is essentially coming up with a good idea and executing it, and then at some point the business either becomes successful or it doesn't. In reality there are many stages in-between, and it's never easy to say if a business has been successful or not, depending on the goals you set. It's not a failure if you don't give up, and it's not necessarily a success if you keep going.

Whatever the outcome of your business journey, there will certainly be times when you are overwhelmed with challenges and think about giving up. There may be times when you achieve something big and feel like nothing can stop you. Whether you're experiencing highs or lows, they should both be used as a way to push you forward, rather than something that stops you from continuing.

The Business Growth Cycle

Look at your highs or lows as part of your business growth cycle, which goes something like this:

When you're just starting out in business, or even if you're already in business but starting a new venture, it can feel incredibly exciting. The feeling of leaving your 9 to 5 job, making your own decisions and carving out your own financial path can be wonderful. You feel ready to take on the world with your business ideas, and you might be ready to hit the ground running to achieve your success.

Things might start off really well and as the momentum builds, you might wonder what all the fuss about entrepreneurship is about. But there will come a day when things don't quite go to plan, or something unexpected happens that's out of your control. This is when your backup plans A, B and C come into play.

Sometimes it might seem that problems and issues all come at once, and you feel overwhelmed with the number of fires you need to fight. On top of this, you're still trying to keep it together for your family and be a parent to the kids. There will be times where challenges at work, combined with the kids just not playing ball, might really get to you and make you feel like you want to give up on everything. *You can't give up, it's not even a choice, so you have to battle on.* With persistence and sheer grit, you put out the fires one by one and things calm down, operations return to normality (whatever normality even means now), and you're best friends with your kids again. Your business starts to build momentum and life is good once more.

This whole cycle will happen again and again, the constant switch between excitement, optimism, fighting fires and overcoming challenges, large and small. After a few of these major highs and major lows, you start to realise this is the normality of running a business. As you build your emotional, mental and physical resilience after each episode of putting out a set of fires, you realise that every time you come out of a tough and challenging time, you've become stronger and more experienced. It's like going to the gym. After a hard session your body feels bruised and battered, but as you recover you've become a slightly stronger, fitter person than before.

Each time you come out of these challenging cycles, you build confidence, you get braver and you start setting your sights on bigger goals (where no doubt you will meet even more challenging times). Your persistence and growing confidence will be right there to help you overcome those too and get to the next level.

> **"EACH TIME YOU EXPERIENCE TOUGH AND CHALLENGING SITUATIONS IT MEANS YOU'RE ABOUT TO LEVEL UP."**

Listening to others

During these growth cycles, you will no doubt come across people who want to give you their opinions and advice. There's nothing wrong with that - getting a different point of view is important, particularly when you're going through challenging times. However, there are a few critical things to be conscious of when taking advice from others.

- Does the person giving the advice have your business' interests at heart?
- Do they fully understand your circumstances?
- Are they basing their advice purely on their own strengths and weaknesses instead of yours?
- It's sad to say that whilst most of the people around you should have your best interests at heart, not all will. Some may not want to see you succeed, not because they're malicious but because they don't want to be left behind. They may want to keep you close because they think they will lose you if you succeed.

It's always great to have people around you who want to offer their help, advice and opinions. Most of the time it shows that they care and are willing to give up some of their own time to help you. Whatever advice you do get, only follow the bits that make sense to you and your particular circumstances, and drive your business forward.

QUICK STORY

In the early years, I would often ask for feedback from friends and family. Being young, I took their feedback as gospel and acted on that feedback. Some friends would try to be helpful and gave me lots of details, and others would give me an overall summary of what they thought. After a while, it became quite tedious to constantly change my product to what they thought was good or bad. Eventually I got to a point where I had lost the identity of my own product. It had changed so much that I had forgotten what my own focus and goal was.

I realised that whilst most of the feedback was given based on good intentions, much of it was given without taking into account the full spectrum of considerations, including who my target audience was, similar products that were already out there and pricing points. I had changed my product based on their opinion alone and forgotten what I was trying to achieve. I ended up reverting back to my original product.

Today, as always, I welcome feedback on my new projects but I also analyse it and only take the parts that truly make sense to my business and original goals.

Be totally self aware

When you're making decisions that affect your business and family, you have to be 100 per cent honest with yourself and base your decisions on your own abilities. Developing a strong sense of self-awareness is critical to building a successful business as a parent. Business and life are just a series of decisions – sometimes you make good ones and sometimes you make bad ones. You base your decisions on many factors, but mainly your confidence in yourself and in other people around you. Always aim to push beyond your own limits – it's how you grow – but understand your own strengths and weaknesses, and what those limits are. This can make the difference between a good decision and a bad one.

It's been said that true entrepreneurs take risks, but what that really means is *calculated* risks. Successful entrepreneurs make decisions based on their own experience, knowledge and confidence in themselves or the people that work with them. That confidence is built on a series of growth cycles – overcoming challenging times, learning from them and understanding their own strengths.

> **BE 100 PER CENT HONEST WITH YOURSELF AND DON'T DO ANYTHING THAT YOU HAVE VERY LITTLE CONFIDENCE IN**

Only you know how good or bad you are at something. Push those limits by all means, but there's a difference between going just beyond your limits and doing something you have very little experience in.

There was a time, very early in my business career, when I made decisions based purely on what result I wanted to achieve, rather than considering how possible they actually were. I was young and sometimes decided to blindly do something in the hope that I'd figure out a way to make it work at some point. Whilst this strategy sometimes did work, it was challenging and put me in some sticky situations. Most decisions made on that premise usually did not end well. As I grew wiser, more experienced in business and understood myself better, I realised that 'taking a leap of faith' actually means understanding whether you're ready to make the leap, what you're leaping from, and how far the leap is, not just what you're leaping to.

20

MANAGING FRIENDSHIPS

By the time I started my first business I already had a few side hustles, so I'd developed a work ethic that most of my friends didn't yet have. Whilst they were enjoying their evenings chilling out and watching TV, playing video games or going out, I was busy building my business after my normal 9 to 5 job. Don't get me wrong – I loved to socialise, but I just didn't do it as often as my friends did. I didn't feel left out, I felt like I was adding value to my life.

With that slight difference in attitude, most of my friends couldn't understand why I was working in the evenings after being at work all day, or why I didn't want to join them every time they invited me out. I usually only showed my face on special occasions, at people's birthdays, Christmas, and other big meet-ups. I saw my friends enough, just not all the time.

Friends don't always get what you're trying to do

It can be difficult to articulate what you're trying to do and what your goals are to friends who aren't at the same stage in life where they want to build something for themselves. I used to have some crazy business ideas, many of which would never come to fruition (even I knew that), but I would at least try to deliver a version of it.

Some of my friends used to mock my business ideas and think I was just dreaming, or that I was wasting my time. On many occasions they were right, some of my ideas were so out there that I just didn't have the resources, skills or experience at the time to deliver them. However, looking back, every time I tried a business idea and failed, I was moving forwards because I was learning from my mistakes. Even to this day, with the businesses I am involved in, I have used all the things I learned from my mistakes in those early years of trying start a business.

Consider which friends to share new ideas with

Most of us know what a good friend should look like, but when it comes to telling friends about your ideas, and specifically how they react to you starting a business, not all of them will be able to offer the support and encouragement you need. Limit discussions about your business plans to those who will help you to achieve your goals, even if this is just emotional support.

We all have friends who support us 100 per cent, no matter what, because they believe in us. These are the friends who lift your spirits during those low points of starting a business. Whether they understand your business idea or not, they fully understand that you have a goal and you want to achieve it. They may not be able to help you directly with your business, but they will support you and your family or the people around you. These friends are there for a chat when you need it, but also understand that you need time to work on your business. They don't blame you for not calling because they know you're chasing your dreams. Keep these types of friends close by – they are your pillars of support and you need them at every stage of your journey, not just in business but also in life. Don't forget to reach out to them once in a while and tell them how much you appreciate them. These people are your friends unconditionally, whether you make it in business or not.

Other friends may tell you your business idea sucks, *because it actually might suck*. Whilst it may be hard to hear that someone doesn't like your idea, it can be good to have some constructive feedback. These friends might give a reason why your idea won't work and may even suggest how to improve it. You need this type of feedback to constantly improve. Not everyone's going to love your idea, and that's a good thing because you need external input to make your product or service better, especially if the person giving the feedback falls into your target market.

Then there are those friends that appear to support you, but don't really believe or agree with what you are doing and secretly think you're wasting your time. That's fine. Not everyone will see or understand your vision – it's *your vision* after all – but it's best to be careful not to over share all of your ideas with this group of friends. Some may even appear to support you, and might think your idea is good, but they want to see how it pans out before deciding if they want to emotionally support you. Usually investing too much time in telling this group your idea and your business vision might be a waste, since you're never going to get the emotional or direct support you need in the early stages of a business.

Finally there are those that tell you that your idea is rubbish to your face, without offering constructive criticism, because they don't want you to be successful – or at least they don't want you to be more successful than they are. This group of people in the early stages of your business can be very dangerous. Your product or service may not be developed enough for you to have a concrete plan to push to market.

At this stage, you might be open to outside influences. When those influences are not in the best interests of your fledgling business, it can cause it harm and hinder your progress. Keep these people at arm's length when it comes to discussing your business idea.

Keeping certain people close is very important. You need those that will give you support and words of encouragement when things get tough. Friends that will give you genuine feedback, whether your idea is good or bad, are also invaluable because they want you to succeed. You also need friends that won't be counting how many times you made it to social occasions, because they know you're busy chasing your dreams. Keep those friends with you throughout your journey.

> **"NOT ALL OF YOUR FRIENDS WILL BE ABLE TO GIVE THE RIGHT KIND OF SUPPORT YOU NEED FOR YOUR FLEDGLING BUSINESS – RECOGNISE WHICH ONES TO CONFIDE IN."**

Maintaining good friendships as a parent

If you are lucky enough to have the kind of friends that can offer you support that helps you grow, you need to keep these friends close. It's much easier to find the time to build these friendships when you don't have a family, but when you are starting or running a business as a parent, quite naturally you will spend any spare time that isn't working on your business, with your family. So where do you find the time to spend with friends? In chapter 8 I wrote about layering and stacking tasks to save time, and the same can be done with managing friendships too. If there is any overlap with family or business events that could involve friends it's a great idea to combine events and activities.

QUICK STORY

When I left high school, the group of friends I was closest to went our separate ways for university. Throughout those university years we didn't keep in touch and I thought that everyone had moved on and we wouldn't see each other again. After university, one of the friends reached out to organise a small reunion and the four of us went out for a drink at Christmas. For the next few years that became the tradition. No matter where we all were in the country, the four of us would meet up at Christmas. This carried on until one by one, we got married and the original four became eight with our other halves. We were lucky that we also entered parenthood around the same time and the group of eight friends turned in seventeen of us with all the kids, so naturally our kids played together and the adults were still able to spend time with each other. We were able to layer our social time on top of some of our family time; we were spending time with the kids but also with friends. I was also lucky that one of the friends also started his own property business, so we had even more in common and did some deals together. Quite often we layered family time on top of a business catch up.

For the friends I couldn't physically spend time with, social media played a vital role in keeping connected with people who I highly valued as a friend and want to continue building a strong friendship with. Whilst many people already know social media should never be a replacement for real life interactions, in chapter 24, I cover the importance of value-added social media where it should act as an extension of your life and not a replacement, and how it can help you continue to build strong friendships when there are physical limitations, like distance and time.

Section Three

RUNNING YOUR BUSINESS

21

GET OUT OF YOUR COMFORT ZONE TO GROW YOUR BUSINESS

When you're about to become a parent for the first time, you prepare yourself by reading all kinds of parenting books, you attend antenatal classes and floods of advice comes in from friends and family, and even from people who *don't even have kids*. Even though you think you're well prepared, the day your baby arrives, it hits you like a ton of bricks. *You're a parent!* Another human being's life depends on you and everything that you've read and learnt no longer matters because despite all the advice, a thousand new small issues you hadn't anticipated arise and you're left to deal with them on your own, without a safety net. The books and classes teach you all the big parenting theory stuff, but they don't teach you how to go to work stinking of baby puke. Nor do they teach you how to deal with the exploding poo that shoots not only out of the nappy, but up and out the back of your baby's neck while you're stood in the middle of the supermarket. And they definitely don't teach you what to do when your two-year-old abseils down the curtains and you end up in A&E until 2 am, or how to concentrate on work the next day.

Somehow, incredibly, you manage and you deal with it, and after each exploding nappy, tantrum and sleepless night, you learn and you grow. Then if you are crazy enough to have another child, you take all those things in your stride, because you know exactly how to deal with it. You know that it's not the end of the world to sit in meetings stinking of baby puke. You are prepared for the exploding nappy with three extra changes of clothes. And you don't end up in A&E quite as often, because you fit blinds instead of curtains. The point is, you may begin in a totally uncomfortable situation, but the uncomfortable becomes comfortable because your comfort zone has expanded.

> **YOU NEED TO CHALLENGE YOURSELF IN ORDER TO GROW YOUR BUSINESS.**

This is exactly what business is about. It's about throwing yourself into uncomfortable situations that you learn to get out of and control, and then the next time they happen you are more prepared. There are some remarkable similarities between parenting and business, and the skills you pick up as a parent can certainly be transferred to starting and running a business too. After all, your business is also your baby.

QUICK STORY

I've had my fair share of lows, where I've had to learn quickly and dig myself out of a sticky situation. The most memorable was when I first became involved in property development.

Along with my consultancy and marketing businesses, I started working alongside an established property developer who had built hundreds of apartments in the UK. I was already connected to many property brokers and agents through networking for my marketing businesses and was able to generate leads. I was invited to be a non-executive director and given the role of finding new development opportunities, acquiring land on behalf of the company and seeing deals through.

There was one particular deal where the land was seemingly up for sale by an agent but was too big for us. It was £12 million and was out of our league - I was certainly outside of my comfort zone. But I had another property contact who was interested in the land, and as I had already built up a strong relationship with the agent selling the land, I was asked to make an introduction and to bridge the initial communication.

As we started to build some dialogue with the agent, I got a mysterious phone call. The chap at the other end of the line told me he was the real owner of the land. He sounded a little threatening and told me to stay away from any dealings with his land. He also went on to say that if he lost any money from it he would come after me and send his people down to my house to 'sort me out'.

Clearly there was something untoward with that piece of land and the ownership was questionable. He didn't want me or anyone else sniffing around, and I wasn't quite sure why, but I wasn't going to pursue it further. In the marketing and technology consulting business, we don't have these kinds of conversations, so I was pretty shocked. I had no idea what to say to him. He put the phone down and I never heard from the agent again.

I had expanded my business experience and knowledge from marketing and technology consulting to property development through a really uncomfortable and stressful situation, but it pushed me out of my normal comfort zone. I learnt from it, and what was previously unchartered territory then became the norm. I became comfortable discussing land deals of that size and I learnt to do more due diligence, spot potential issues and to steer away from questionable property deals.

Push your limits

At the beginning of your business journey, you can create situations that are uncomfortable but controllable. You can do this by stretching your limits a bit at a time and going a little further than you've ever been.

Let's say you have a catering business and you usually cater for small events like parties or small businesses. The real money is in big events, weddings and corporate functions, but you're not sure if you can handle such a large event. The first time you attempt one, it might be stressful, you might have to earn next to nothing just to land the contract, and you might need to do a lot of the work yourself, working through several nights to make the event work. It might be the toughest thing that you've done in your life, but once you've done it, and you understand and learn from any mistakes, you've got experience catering for big events. The next time you do it, you can charge more, you can hire a team to help you, and you'll be more organised with better processes and logistics in place. Now you're no longer a smaller caterer, you're a big event caterer – and all it took was pushing your boundaries and getting out of your comfort zone.

Growing is uncomfortable. But without that pain, you can't grow at all. These are called growing pains and they happen to all businesses, big and small.

22

PROMOTING AND MARKETING YOUR BUSINESS

There are many elements to a good business operation. At the core of your business is your product and service, but it's not enough just to have this. You need all the other functions wrapped around it to make your product or service ready for market. Whether you are running a business and juggling family or not, one of the most important wrappers is sales and marketing. If you don't get this bit right, no one's going to buy your product or service.

QUICK STORY

As a teenager, and in my adult life, I had many side hustles (see chapter 3) but throughout all these little ventures there was one skill I didn't realise I'd been developing – sales and marketing.

I developed logos, packaging, leaflets, brochures and web banners for online auctions. I wrote email sales copy and built contact lists. I didn't know what I was actually doing at the time, all I knew was I needed to sell my products and I did what I thought was necessary to sell them. I didn't know how to use design software so I learnt through trial and error. I didn't know how to develop sales copy, so I'd read about it and test which email copy would sell more products and which wouldn't, and which words and phrases would work better than others. Even at a young age, working in my parents' restaurant business, I had developed a way of speaking to customers that got the best out of them and presented what I wanted to say in the right light. I developed a way to have valuable conversations with people.

All of those skills were invaluable as I became a freelance marketer, moved on to building a digital marketing agency and set up as a digital marketing consultant, advising small and large companies how to grow their digital marketing.

Starting a conversation

Marketing, especially in this digital age, changes constantly. Every day in fact. Technology has changed the way that consumers and businesses buy and sell products and services. It's a fast moving world – if you're not paying attention to the changing landscape of technology, you'll get left behind.

One thing that will never change – and hasn't changed since I was a teenager selling console games to my school friends – is that no matter how advanced technology gets, what new digital platforms society adopts, or what products and services you're selling, sales and marketing is just a conversation. That conversation might not be face to face, but all you are trying to establish is rapport with your customers. It doesn't matter how that takes place, whether it's over the phone, in person, on a website, in a social media post or in an email, what you need to do is start that conversation. These days, people get so wrapped up in the technical side and techniques of sales and marketing that they forget about the core values of their message. To start the conversation about your product or service, you need to establish these three things:

- **WHERE** do you find your customers?
- **WHAT** are the real benefits of your products and services for customers?

- **HOW** do you deliver your products and services and how much does it cost?

Where are your customers?

You can't have a conversation with your potential customers if you don't know where they are. As well as establishing your customer persona, you need to find out where to get in front of your potential customers.

For example, if you wanted to promote an event aimed at students, you might want to give out leaflets and flyers outside places where students hang out the most, perhaps outside university campus buildings, student unions or perhaps in student bars. Of course, today with all the digital platforms, it's much easier to reach people online.

TOPPs Analysis is a useful tool, which helps you identify where your customers are 'hanging out'. To conduct a TOPPs analysis with your target customer in mind, you just need make a small list (about five items should do) under each of the headings shown below. These are the places and areas you need to 'hang out' (sometimes digitally), as this is where your target customers are spending their time. TOPPs stands for:

Tools and Topics

Organisations

People

Publications

For example, if you sell a no-spill beaker for toddlers, your target market will be parents with young kids. To reach them, you might want to run some ads on social media or banner ads on certain websites, so you need to know where to target them. Using TOPPs, under each heading write down a list of interests that these parents might follow.

Under Tools and Topics you might want to write down topics that parents with young kids could be interested in, such as sleep training, or online tools and guides like *Baby Centre* which is a website packed full of guides and resources for new parents. Under Organisations you might want to write down brands that parents buy for their children, such as Mothercare, PlaySkool, Mamas and Papas, MaxiCosi. Under People you could write down the characters that their children follow, such as those from Disney, Mr Tumble, or any other characters that they watch on TV or online. Under Publications you might want to write down any magazines or online forums, such as mumsnet.

Once you've got your information, this will form your target list – what your target audience is interested in and where they're hanging out. On social media you can then target these individuals based on their interests. Most social media platforms allow you to place targeted ads aimed at specific interests, such as the brands, tools and the people in your TOPPs analysis.

In the case of publications, you can go directly into forums such as mumsnet and get involved with the community. You shouldn't try to sell directly within the forums as there are usually strict guidelines on selling services. Instead, you can slowly introduce your product from a neutral angle, or you can ask the moderators if there are any advertising opportunities such as banner ads.

With this targeting, you can now start conversations in the right environment and reach potential customers.

What are the benefits to your customers?

When you're starting or running your business in the early years, no doubt you will be very excited to show people your product or service in all its glory. But here's a little known fact: customers don't care about anything other than the benefits or value a product or service is going to create for them.

Whoever your internet service provider is, you use them because the connection speed is fast and the price is reasonable. But the moment the system slows down or the connection starts to drop repeatedly, you'll consider moving to another provider who can give you a better service. People perceive branding to be a powerful marketing tool and it can be, but your product or service has also got to live up to the brand's promise and quality.

It's the same for big brands like Apple, Nike or Audi - all huge brands with a loyal following. But the moment their products drop below the quality or standard their customers and followers expect from them, they start moving to other equally high quality brands like, Samsung, Adidas or Mercedes. People only follow brands if the product lives up to the brand's high standards.

> **"THINK ABOUT THE NEEDS OF YOUR TARGET AUDIENCE FIRST AND WHAT THEY NEED, RATHER THAN WHAT YOU OFFER."**

Describe your product and service with the benefit and value first, followed by what your product actually is. People don't care about what you've got to sell until they know what it's going to do for them.

Let's use the example of the toddler non-spill sippy cup mentioned earlier. Most businesses would market this product with: 'The no-spill sippy cup stops your toddler from spilling their drink, comes in three bright colours, has two durable handles and a lid. It's easy to clean and dishwasher proof – get yours today!'

With the benefit and value upfront it might read like this: 'Tired of cleaning up your toddler's drink spills? Are your rugs and carpets getting a little worn? Our no-spill sippy cup stops your toddler from spilling their drink, comes in three bright colours, has two durable handles and a lid. It's easy to clean, dishwasher proof and includes free next day delivery – get yours today!'

The difference here is that we've grabbed the customer's attention in the first five seconds with the value and benefit that they are looking for.

When I ask my five year old whether she wants to go somewhere new, instead of telling her the name of the place, I start with what fun she could have there, what friends might be there and how exciting the place is. At this stage, the venue is irrelevant, as she has already bought into the fun, friends and excitement.

> **TELL THE CUSTOMER WHAT THE VALUE OR BENEFIT TO THEM IS FIRST, FOLLOWED BY WHAT YOUR PRODUCT AND SERVICE OFFERING IS.**

How do they get it and how much does it cost?

You've identified where your potential audience is. You've figured out how to convey your product messaging. Now you need to persuade your customers to buy. The world is saturated with fantastic products and services, as a society we really are spoilt for choice in almost all areas of life. If you want to buy a new TV, you literally have thousands of options to choose from. So how do you make your product or service stand out? It really comes down to two things – price and convenience.

Price is the obvious one – if you sell an identical product or service to a competitor and your competitor sells it at a lower price, the obvious choice for the customer would be to buy from your competitor. But a lower price usually comes with some consequences in the majority of cases. What if, at the lower price, the customer would have to wait seven days before they can get their product delivered? It depends on how urgently the customer needs the product and the value the customer places on speed of delivery. Let's say the customer needs the product in the next two days and you can deliver your product the next day, but for 15 per cent more than your competitor. The extra 15 per cent is a small price to pay to get your product quickly.

One example of this is Amazon. Quite often, Amazon products available on Prime come at a slightly higher price. The price increase is usually negligible, between 5-15 per cent, but to be able to get their purchase the next day, many people would pay the premium for the speed. This is a prime example (no pun intended) of how the combination of price and convenience is the key to winning a sale. A low price doesn't always guarantee a sale – the buying journey and experience also makes a big difference.

Convenience is as important as price in today's society. PayPal is an example of this. Most online businesses that offer PayPal as one of their payment methods know most people will pay via PayPal when given the option. Given the choice between having to dig your wallet out and manually type in the card numbers into the payment screen, or just punching in your PayPal username and password, most customers would choose the latter.

Depending on what product or service you're selling, think about how you distribute and sell it, and think carefully about the buying experience for your customers, focusing on making the process as easy as possible. All it takes is one too many screens, questions or steps to put people off buying from you. Consider the following points:

- If you are selling a product online, how quick is your checkout process?
- Are you asking for anything unnecessary?
- Is it essential for them to login to be able to buy anything?
- If you are selling something physical in a retail shop, how easy is it for people to find your products?
- Is there a way you could automate their payments?
- If you are selling a service, what's the quickest way customers can sign up?
- Do they have to do it in person?
- Could they sign an agreement or contract online using the many legally binding digital signature services?

- Do you have automations in place to keep customers posted on the service you provide?

Whatever product and service you are offering, try to take away as much friction at every level as possible. People love lower prices but they will also pay for convenience.

23

THE POWER OF PERCEPTION

In business, perception is important. It doesn't matter how good your product or service is, at the end of the day it comes down to what other people, and specifically your potential customers, think of it.

You might have been told as you grew up: 'It doesn't matter what other people think of you, as long as you are happy that's all that counts'. While being comfortable with yourself and not doing things to please others may be an admirable trait in life, in business you need others to like what you and your business have to offer, otherwise they just won't buy from you.

Even when I was working for an employer, I saw so many talented colleagues get left behind, not getting promotions and pay rises because they just didn't know how to sell them-selves. Selling yourself isn't about bragging about how good your work is, it's about showcasing what you've done in the most positive light. You don't have to be arrogant, but you do have to tell people what you've done and achieved, because if you don't, they simply won't notice.

Good perception of what you have to offer is powerful. It can turn a mediocre product into a business, and it can turn a great product into a huge success. In order to build continual success, good perception needs to be backed up by a good product or service.

QUICK STORY

When I invested in my first tech start-up, Gurooo, the app was marketed so well that public perception was better than the product itself. The promise of the app was so good, and we focused so much on perception and branding, that the app itself didn't live up to the hype. We were so worried that we wouldn't get enough users that we spent too much time pre-promoting it and building up hype instead of first focusing on developing a world class product. When we finally launched the beta version, it just didn't do as well as we hoped, and we encountered lots of technical problems because it didn't live up to the expectations of the marketing.

On the flip side, when I had the digital marketing agency business, we organically developed a web development team that would work alongside our marketing teams. Being able to develop high-end websites combined with our digital marketing expertise meant we were developing a much more superior product than our competitors, who were at the time either just offering web development or digital marketing. The problem was, we were so focused on the digital marketing product that we didn't push the web development business. This turned into dozens of missed opportunities as some of our clients went to other web development agencies. The perception of our business was so focused around our digital marketing product that people didn't think web development was a service we offered, resulting in tens of thousands of pounds of missed revenue.

Developing a great perception of your products, services and business isn't a one-time project. It's an ongoing and long-term commitment to how you communicate with the outside world. It doesn't just sit with the marketing remit, it's at management level with you, across all your staff and everything your business touches.

Be clear about what you actually do

If perception is about how people see you and your business, then being able to quickly communicate what you do in the right tone, and from the right angle, is important. This is how the perception begins.

This might sound odd, but because I'm involved in running and operating so many different types of marketing, technology, property and consulting businesses, it was only until recently that my wife was able to quickly describe what I do for a living when anyone would ask her. For many people who run a single business it might be as easy as 'I run an IT business', 'I own a restaurant' or 'I have a web design business', but it was difficult for her to cram everything I do into a short sentence.

Why is this important? If people can't quickly explain what you do, the chances are they probably also can't quickly explain how you might be able to help someone solve a problem with your product or service. If they can't see or understand what you do, they can't recommend you to others.

You need to be able to describe what you do in a quick sentence within 30 seconds. Many call this the 'Elevator Pitch', which is a clear message that outlines what it is your business does and what its mission is. It's typically about 30 seconds long, because it refers to the time it takes people to ride from the top to the bottom of a building in an elevator. The 'Elevator Pitch' mostly fits in an investment context where, if you met an investor in the elevator, you would have 30 seconds to describe what it is your business does to persuade them to invest.

However, being able to describe your business in 30 seconds to anyone, not just investors, will help you communicate easily and allow people to talk about what you do with ease.

What does 'being the best' mean?

Once you have developed your elevator pitch, you then need to make sure value is woven into it. Many people might be tempted to mention that they are 'the best' in their market but you don't even have to be the best in the market to be successful. Getting your potential customers to want to buy from you is more about making them feel your product or service is right for their needs than it is about being the best. 'Best' will mean different things to different people. It could mean best in price, best in quality, best in speed, or best in volume. One customer that wants a best in price may not necessarily expect best in quality, and one that wants best in quality may not want best in volume.

There's no need to boast about your business either, let the facts speak for themselves. Let's say you are selling an IT support service: '*We offer the best high quality IT Support service in the market. Our engineers are here to solve your technical issues, all at a low monthly subscription of £100 per month. Join today!*' This statement doesn't really say much about your IT Support business. Who says it's the best?

Instead this angle assures the reader: '*We handle your business' IT headaches and monitor your systems 24/7, so you can focus on growing your business, all for the price of your daily cup of coffee. Join over 800 businesses today and say goodbye to technical headaches!*'

In the second statement, we are addressing the prospect's technical worries straight away so they know they can get on with growing their business. Then we break down that monthly cost to a daily figure and put it into perspective of just over £3 per day. Finally we add some trust and assurance that we already handle IT support for over 800 other businesses – if they trust us, why shouldn't you?

> **CHANGING HOW YOU ARE PERCEIVED IN YOUR MARKETING MESSAGING IS THE DIFFERENCE BETWEEN GETTING A NEW CLIENT OR NOT.**

Constant communication of your core business messaging in everything you do is the key to being perceived in the right light. It's about integrating your achievements, case studies and facts into *every* business conversation and marketing message.

24

USING VALUE-ADDED SOCIAL MEDIA

Social media sometimes gets bad press, mainly because certain bodies believe people are wasting their time watching funny cat videos, stalking their exes or generally doing things that add no value. Whilst this might actually be the case for many people, social media can also be an extremely powerful tool for the entrepreneur.

Social media has always played an important role in my business and personal life. Most people are already aware of this, but I realised that I had to be responsible about how I use social media, and to actively regulate the time I spend on the various platforms. I found that it can be very easy to let it take over my life, but when used with value in mind, it can be a vital and valuable part of my life.

Getting inspiration and ideas

You can use various platforms as a way to get inspiration and ideas for your business. Sometimes you don't know what you don't know, so when browsing social media and connecting with people, you can discover things you would never have thought about learning. Working in both property and technology, social media provides me with a way to find out about up-and-coming property hot spots. Posts and shares from other property professionals give me insight into what's happening in other areas of the property world directly on the ground. Sometimes when you read articles in publications or watch things on the news, it can paint a biased and edited version of what is going on. When you hear it directly from the people that are in the game, you see the reality.

In my technology and marketing businesses, I can stay ahead of the game by seeing what the tech giants are doing, not from the brand themselves but from the people who worked for them. The engineers, marketing people or even the executives will discuss certain topics, often before mainstream media catches on and gets around to writing an article about it. Social media can help you spot trends to educate your own clients on what might happen in your sector. You can use these tools to generate more leads, sales and revenue and to stay ahead of your competition.

Social media tools can sometimes help you discover things that perhaps you didn't know about being a parent, too. Parent forums can keep you in the loop at your child's school, and keep you informed about new products and services that help make life as a parent easier, and you might even find time- and cost-saving ideas and tips.

Staying connected

Being a parent and running a business can get lonely at times. You dedicate so much of your time to building your business and spending time with your family that your social life can take a bit of a back seat.

Social media allows you to stay in touch with friends and family when you can't physically find the time to meet them. Being able to keep in touch with a wider circle of friends is also important and social media allows you to do that when you can't spend time in a room with them. Of course, it's not a substitute for seeing friends in person, but it can help when you are buried in the momentum of working on your new business.

> "SOCIAL MEDIA CAN BE A GREAT EXTENSION OF YOUR REAL WORLD SOCIAL INTERACTIONS, BUT NOT A REPLACEMENT."

It's a common topic of discussion - people become depressed because of social media, and allow themselves to become addicted and slowly let online interactions replace real world interactions. It's become such an issue in society that even schools address the topic with kids from a young age.

However, when you use social media as part of your real world friendships it can form a powerful way to be even closer to friends - it allows you to continue being with them in their life even after you have seen them in person. Interacting and engaging in the things they share enables you to be part of their world and them in yours. This brings people together even more when done in moderation.

When you are deep in your business and spending time with your family, so can't physically be with friends in person, social media allows you to catch-up on what they're doing and still be part of their life.

QUICK STORY

Some years ago I was on holiday in Hong Kong with my family. I had posted photos of us at various spots in the city when I got a message on Facebook from an old high school friend. It turned out he was also visiting Hong Kong with his family. We organised to meet up for lunch. Who would have thought after 15 years of not seeing each other in person, since we both left school and went our separate ways, that social media would reunite us on the other side of the planet?

Sharing your journey

When you're focusing on your business and have less time to see friends, it's difficult to keep them up to speed with what you're doing. I find that it's important to involve some of your friends in what you are doing, even if it is only a few close ones. If you don't keep them in the loop, you can quickly distance yourself from them. One day you're starting something and then the next time you see them you're a fully-fledged entrepreneur – this might make it seem like you've changed when really you haven't.

By involving friends throughout my business journey, not only do they know what I'm up to, but I also get feedback much more easily when I ask for it, because they see another side of me that perhaps I wouldn't usually show. You don't need to share everything, just some of your highs and lows. Many people only share the good side of their life, the part that's positive and makes it look like everything's perfect. Sharing some of the not-so-glossy parts of your journey is also important – it shows your friends you're not just showing off, but you are sharing some of your vulnerabilities, which makes you a more rounded person.

The most important part of sharing your business journey on social media with your friends, is to remember not to treat them as potential customers. Your friends are there to listen, watch and go on your business journey together with you – they don't want to be sold to. It changes the relationship completely, and can damage a good friendship.

Building and widening your network

Social media is a scalable way to increase your own personal network. In 'real life' there is only a finite amount of time you can spend physically networking and going out to meet new people in both life and business.

> "WHEN USED IN THE RIGHT WAY, SOCIAL MEDIA CAN BE A POWERFUL TOOL TO HELP EXTEND YOUR OWN SOCIAL LIFE AND MAKE NEW BUSINESS CONNECTIONS."

On social media, you can tap into a whole new network of people on various social platforms that you wouldn't normally be able to connect with.

QUICK STORY

I have met many people on different social media platforms that I definitely wouldn't have been able to meet in real life. For the property business, I was able to interact with other developers, landowners and agents. They were able to give me insider tips before property and land went to market, or suggest trends in certain areas that perhaps I wouldn't have heard about had I not met these people on social media.

In the technology and marketing business, I have acquired more new business and deals, and received more recommendations via people I've never actually met using social media than I have in person. I have clients on the other side of the planet who have continued to refer others to me as clients. I've also been able to recruit staff via social media, and as most of our technology and marketing work is all in the cloud, I have an even better chance of tapping into talent and experience without the constraints of location. Some of my team span several cities in the UK. I also have teams spread across other countries that help service clients in other time zones that I have never met in person, but speak to on a daily basis. This is the power of social media and the cloud – all you need is an internet connection to be able to tap into all this talent, experience and knowledge.

25

WORRYING IS A WASTE OF TIME

From the moment your first child arrives, as a parent you never stop worrying. The list of worries is endless - worrying about them getting ill or hurt, worrying if you are teaching or guiding them enough or too much, worrying if they are happy or getting bullied at school, to name but a few.

When you decide to leave the comforts of your 9 to 5 job and venture out into the world of business on your own, there is even more worry to deal with - how to get more customers, worrying about your overheads, worrying about paying staff, worrying about how to pay yourself and worrying about competitors stealing your customers.

As a parent entrepreneur, the stress of trying to be a good parent and run a business at the same time can be really overwhelming. In the years since I've become a parent running businesses, there have been several times when I have felt so much pressure and stress that it affected my health, and a few times I thought I was having a mini stroke.

QUICK STORY

During a particularly stressful period of time, the people of the UK voted to leave the EU and I lost a large client that had been acquired by another company based in Germany. The new parent company decided to cut all UK supplier contracts and to award the contracts to local suppliers instead. At the same time, some of my investors whose own businesses were also going through a challenging period due to the UK leaving the EU, pulled some of their investment. I was not in a good place and I was constantly worrying. It seemed as if one bad thing was happening after another.

After weeks of constant worry about what else might go wrong, the penny dropped one day while I was taking my then 5-year-old daughter to school. As we were stuck in traffic she told me she was worried about going in to school that day. *What has a 5 year old got to worry about?* I wondered. She told me that she was worried her friends wouldn't think her new school skirt was beautiful. I smiled and told her that she looked lovely, but as long as she liked the skirt herself and it made her feel confident wearing it, it didn't matter what other people thought. It seemed a very cute and trivial concern to me, but then I suddenly realised: whilst it seemed trivial *to me*, it was in fact a big deal *to her*, and the more she made it a big deal, the more worried she became.

After our little chat, I looked at my own situation. Whilst my worries seemed stressful to me, to others looking in they may have seemed relatively trivial. I had been in business several years and I had been in worse situations. I had my family, I had my health and I was surrounded by loved ones. I had built things from nothing before, and if I lost it all, I could just do it again. As long as I was confident in my own ability, I could figure a way out.

Turn a negative into a positive

Sometimes we can overthink things. We forget the most basic of principles and it can take a small reminder (in this case, my 5-year-old) to show us that life and business are very simple. Have faith in your own abilities – as long as you have your health and determination, you can make anything happen. Worrying wastes valuable time and energy. Instead of thinking about the bad things that 'could' happen, try to channel that energy into solving the problem. Make good and positive things happen instead.

It can be difficult to see the positives when you're going through a challenging situation. An exercise I often do when everything is seemingly going wrong, is to ask myself this one question; 'Am I going to die because of this?' and so far the answer is always 'No'. As soon as I ask myself this, I gain some perspective on the situation and it clears my mind to focus on the lessons I can take from this, and turn them into positive actions.

> **WORRY AND STRESS JUST KILLS TIME AND MOTIVATION. CHANNEL THAT TIME AND ENERGY INTO ACTIONS THAT MOVE YOUR LIFE FORWARD.**

Get worries off your chest

This might seem pretty obvious to most, but surprisingly most people don't do it. Quite often, most of our worries and concerns can be solved simply by talking to someone. I've found that when you keep your worries and concerns cooped up inside, they start to build up, and whatever you were worried about becomes much bigger than it really is. Whilst you might not want to overburden others with the details, simply telling someone about what's on your mind could be enough to ease the situation.

I often try to verbalise what's in my head and talk to a select few trusted friends and colleagues, and sometimes they come back with some really good advice or a slightly different angle on the situation, and that alone is enough to ease things in my head. I keep it brief and I don't share the intimate details, but just letting someone else know what's going on in your head releases some of the pressure.

If you are lucky enough to have a trusted friend, colleague or family member to talk to, that makes things much easier. But if you don't want to share your concerns with the people around you, hiring a coach to be that soundboard can really help make your business and family life much more worry-free. Coaches can come in different forms. I have an executive coach, he isn't there to just listen to my worries and concerns, nor is he an expert in business or parenting. He helps me by listening to the challenges I'm facing, and asking me the right questions to help me see situations from a different perspective. This often makes me realise something I already knew in my subconscious, but needed to bring to the front of my mind and ease any concerns.

26

MERGING BUSINESS AND FAMILY TIME

When I started my first business in my twenties, I worked all hours of the day and every weekend. It was during that time that I finally knew what it felt like to genuinely love what I did, because working on your own business never feels like work. It feels like an endless hobby that you are addicted to – you want to spend all your time dedicating yourself to your craft.

Being completely absorbed in my business worked well for me before I had a family. But fast-forward ten years and it was a very different scenario. By the time I was in my mid-thirties I had started, partnered with investors and sold a few businesses. I had also failed a bunch of times, lost a load of money and fallen out with several people in the process. Now I had a wife and kids, things were very different. When you have a family you can't spend every waking hour working on your business, because you are now responsible for others who depend on you.

The moment you decide to have kids, you are making an unspoken promise to them that you will care for them and look after their every need, regardless of what circumstances you are in. You are their provider and no matter how tired, stressed or not in the mood you feel, you must be there for them.

Allocating time to your family and business

Starting a new business, is a little like having another child. It needs your attention too – it needs nurturing and investment to grow. As a parent entrepreneur, you suddenly find yourself with two sets of dependants - your children and your new business - both of which are screaming for your attention (quite literally in the case of the kids).

You now need to allocate your time accordingly, and in the fairest way that you can. One way is to ensure that your weekends, or the majority of your weekends, are reserved for your family. It's going to be very difficult to do, because whilst you want to spend time with your family, you'll also be thinking about your business. Get used to it. Stop feeling guilty and embrace that this is now your life.

All work and no play…

The evenings really can be a great time to work, but of course you can't work every single night or you'll burn out. It's important to understand your body and the signals that it's giving you. (In the early years of being a parent I didn't realise I was overstretching myself – I became exhausted, and it cost me nearly a month of downtime to recover.) Make sure you factor in the odd night off – perhaps two out of the five workday evenings – and do something relaxing. Sometimes you just have to do something that requires very little brainpower, like watching a film, going to the gym or meditating.

Your week may not be as straightforward as simply splitting weekdays and weekends, depending on your business, your family structure and set up, but the main thing is to ensure that you allocate and schedule time for your kids, your partner and your business. It is possible to fit everyone in, including a little time for yourself. Plan it all out and communicate your schedule to your kids, partner and everyone involved in your business, so that everyone is on the same page.

You mustn't underestimate the importance of allocating family time. You owe it to them and you owe it to yourself – after all, why are you working so hard if never get to enjoy life with your family?

> **FACTORING IN DEDICATED TIME FOR YOUR PARTNER IS VERY IMPORTANT AND THAT TIME WILL KEEP YOUR RELATIONSHIP HEALTHY.**

Allow room to be flexible

There will be times during the weekend where you get an idea and you're dying to go and test it out, but you can't because the weekend is family time. It's fine to jot down a quick note or a reminder on your phone to look at later in the evening when the kids are in bed. There will also be times during the week at work when your child's school has a special assembly or show, but you feel like you should be focusing on work during the week. That's fine too – running your own business means you don't have to ask to get time off work. You would regret missing a show or assembly – you'll never get those times back, so missing a couple of hours during the day to see your kids is not something any parent should feel guilty about. On those occasions, allow yourself to catch up the time later.

Being a parent entrepreneur is about juggling your own emotions and priorities, and being flexible when you can, rather than blindly setting a schedule and never deviating away from it. When you have a family it's impossible to be totally rigid about time – you have to be flexible within reason.

QUICK STORY

Over the years I've developed a system that works for me. I spend the weekdays on my business, full on, apart from a few hours for dinner with my family, the bath and bedtime routine, and the occasional homework session. As soon as everyone's in bed, I'm back at my desk. For me, there's no better time to work than those twilight hours when there are no disruptions, clients and customers won't be calling, and the kids are asleep in bed. The tranquillity at this time of day is when I come up with my best ideas – sometimes with a cheeky glass of wine to loosen up those brain cells. Of course, wine doesn't need to be involved – the key is feeling relaxed and creative, with no other calls on your time. Good mellow background music or some of your favourite chocolate would be equally helpful!

The weekends are dedicated to my family. For me, Saturday nights are completely off limits – no work whatsoever, regardless of how many new ideas or what deadlines I have. This is family time and that's that. Sometimes it might just mean I can spend extra time with my kids before they sleep. Most importantly, it means I spend quality time with my wife.

27

SELL GENUINE CARE

No matter what type of industry you are in, there will always be competitors who come into the market with a better product, a cheaper service or more appealing promotions. Traditionally, businesses combat this by making their own product even better or by offering their product more cheaply with a better promotion. This is an endless cycle and I've seen it destroy entire industries, where the product quality is so high and the promotions are so good that it creates a price war, leaving businesses with a steadily decreasing profit margin.

The price war trap

When you're starting a new business, you might just be interested in selling as much as you can to begin with. Later on, when you are more established and want to protect your business and customers rather than just creating more sales, this strategy will become a big problem – and by then your overheads will be much higher. Planning out your strategy on how you are going to protect your business against competitors' better products and cheaper services now will save you a lot of stress further down the line. Remember, even if your product is super unique and different now, competitors will try to emulate anything that is working well, diluting the uniqueness of your offering.

With each technological advance, it's becoming more and more easy to emulate the success of others. The fashion industry is a good example of this. There was a time when high fashion houses would bring out a new look and it would take several years for high street and mainstream fashion retailers to bring that look to market. Today, technologically advanced fashion businesses can copy a style from high-end fashion houses within hours of it making its debut on the catwalk.

One of my clients was a chain of laser skin treatment clinics in the UK. Their treatments ranged from laser hair removal to tattoo removal and included a range of high-end skin enhancing and repair treatments. At the peak of their profitability they could charge thousands of pounds for their treatments. Then the laser technology they used made huge advances in its systems and machinery. Whilst the machine still required a skilled operator, it meant that the operator was much more aided and guided by the machine itself. Competitors were able to come into the market with a cheaper workforce, because they no longer needed to hire such a highly skilled operator. More and more competitors were able to offer a similar treatment at lower prices and the price wars began to take over the industry. It became an endless cycle of promotions and giveaways.

Customer service or customer care?

So if it's not just the quality or the price of your product or service that leads the way to success, then what does? The quality of your product or service and its price points are still important factors, but when the industry becomes saturated with high-quality, low-priced offerings you have to find something that others can't replicate.

As a consultant to my clients, I've worked across many industry types including ecommerce, retail and corporate finance, beauty, security, digital, property, education, and many more. The problems of quality and price are the same throughout every industry. The only thing that can't be replicated is customer service and care. It's often frowned upon when people tell business owners that they have to offer good customer service – after all, everyone knows that's important, right? But I'm not just talking about good customer service. I'm talking about exceptional, world class, genuine customer 'care'. This is the only thing that no other competitor can take away from you.

My old business partner once said to me that we needed to be 'irreplaceable'. At the time, he meant we needed to offer a product or service so good that customers wouldn't want to leave. He was right of course, but I also wanted to offer better irreplaceable customer 'care'.

There's an important distinction between service and care. With customer service, you're offering a service that is expected, a good one, something that is on par with, or slightly better than your competitors'. You offer a service that helps the customer with their purchase, and you help them with queries in a polite and efficient manner. That's good customer service.

Customer care is everything you would expect from customer service, but going that extra ten miles. What I mean by this is going above and beyond what is expected of your business, doing something unexpected that will benefit your customer because you genuinely want to help them. Genuine customer care is really trying to understand your customer's life or business needs, and thinking what else you can do to help them.

QUICK STORY

In the early days of running my digital marketing agency we had a big client who was happy with our service, but we were one of the first agencies they had used. They wanted to see what else was out there, so they left us and went to another agency. Six months later, the client came back and hired us again because the other agency wasn't giving them what they wanted. A year or so later, as his business rapidly grew, the client wanted to try another much larger agency and he hired them. The same thing happened, they lasted a few months and he came back to us. He hired in-house managers to try to replicate and manage what we were doing internally. He went through three marketing managers and he eventually came back to us again. He probably didn't even understand why he was coming back to us, but what he was missing from other agencies and managers was that care that no one else could replace.

Genuine care is difficult to replicate. When unexpected things happen, the customers and clients that rely on you know you are there for them in their time of need – that's where your value is.

Care doesn't need to cost money, it doesn't even need to be done in person, it just needs that little bit of thoughtfulness and attention. If you operate a product-based business, ecommerce for example, a simple follow-up email or text to ask customers if their product arrived safely and if they need any help with setting it up, or thanking them by offering a discount voucher off their next purchase, goes a long way. If you are in the service-based industry, but don't see your customers face to face, send periodic emails or communications to ask what challenges they are currently facing, and offer to solve the ones you can help with.

Customer care is a long-term business growth strategy. You don't get instant value back from it, but it will build your brand and business in the long term. I have built my own businesses, built strong relationships with investors and partners and helped my clients forge strong loyalty with their customers, simply by offering genuine care. When the economy goes a bit wobbly and customers are looking to cut their budgets, care stops your business from being one of the first to be cut. When clients and customers want to spend more money, care puts your business at the top of their list. When there are any opportunities, that genuine care that has forged strong relationships and built friendships with your customers and clients puts you in the best possible situation for them to share those opportunities with you.

> **"IT'S REALLY SIMPLE – CARE FOR YOUR CUSTOMERS AND THEY WILL CARE FOR YOU."**

During the early stages of your business, thinking about the things that competitors can't replicate and that make your business stand out will be the key to your growth and survival when the market gets competitive and crowded.

28

THERE ARE OPPORTUNITIES IN EVERY SITUATION

I often tell my daughter 'the world is your oyster', and many of you might have been told the same when you were growing up. Most understand this phrase to simply mean that you can do whatever you want to do, or that there are opportunities everywhere. Whilst this is true, the deeper meaning behind the phrase goes slightly further. You can find oysters very easily, but not every oyster will produce a pearl – the conditions need to be just right. You might have to go through many oysters to find that one pearl - it takes experience to spot which oysters produce pearls and which do not. The same is true with business opportunities – if you look around you will find plenty of inspiration for new ideas, but you need to learn to spot which ones are of value.

QUICK STORY

When I was growing up in my parents restaurant businesses. My mum was a super-passionate restaurant operator and my dad was a great chef. Often when we ate out in other restaurants or cafes, my parents would be really observant about how that business worked – what was on their menu, what ingredients they were using, portion size, the service, the bar, what things might cost, the table settings, and watching the general operations take place. Some things might jump out at them and they would take note, and draw inspiration on how they could increase efficiency, profitability and constantly improve their own restaurants.

Quite often they would even take inspiration from non-restaurant businesses. Once, whilst at a butcher's, my dad watched how the butcher stored the meat and how they arranged it so that it would maximise space, but also make it easier to access quickly at busy times. He took this idea and adapted it for his own restaurant, and managed to increase storage areas in the fridges and freezers. My parents were successful because they were constantly open to new ideas in all types of circumstances.

Looking for inspiration

You don't have to physically be somewhere to get inspiration and find opportunities. Spend a few hours, particularly on social media, filter out all the cat videos and look at what other brands are posting. Most people might skip the ads but you should see advertising and the sponsored posts as sources for new ideas. You can draw a lot of inspiration from what other brands and businesses are posting.

Look at what some of your larger competitors are posting and see how people are reacting to it. What level of customer engagement are they getting? Are they getting a lot of negative or positive comments? Pay attention to what people are saying about the brand or business. There may be something there that you can use and adapt to your own business. Do the same for similar brands that aren't in your industry but target a similar audience.

If you run an ecommerce or online business, take a look at what and how other businesses and brands are selling online. Look at the way they are selling, their promotions, the way they word their posts and what kind of imagery they are using. Look at how people are reacting to them: are people sharing more or commenting more? If people are sharing more, they really like what they see and are recommending it to their friends. If people are commenting, what are they saying about their products? Are they complaining about the quality or delivery of something they ordered? Are they reviewing the product to say how great it is? Are they comparing the product to something similar and saying it is better or worse?

> **IF YOU LOOK HARD ENOUGH, YOU CAN FIND VALUE AND OPPORTUNITIES EVERYWHERE.**

Let's say you sell handmade toys and accessories online. Have a look at some of the well-known children's brands – it doesn't have to be limited to toys, it could be clothing brands or even educational children's brands. Take note of how they post or advertise, their wording and messaging, their imagery or media and the types of promotions they run. Do people react better to discounts or to competitions? You can also take a look at groups focused around parenting and see what people are posting about toys to draw inspiration from the problems or issues that parents have with other toys. You can then tailor your own messaging to address the problems parents have with other brands.

QUICK STORY

As I grew up watching my parents analyse all kinds of businesses to draw inspiration and ideas for their own, I developed this fascination too.

Other than property, I operate in mainly service- and technology-based businesses, but that doesn't mean I can't draw inspiration from other types of business. I look at other businesses and think about how I can make them better by applying my own skillset to them, or how I could adapt some of their processes into my own business. You can literally find nuggets of value and opportunity anywhere if you pay attention.

The digital marketing agency I started with a former business partner early on in my career was a small start-up agency. When pitching to new clients we were constantly competing with much larger agencies that had slicker sales processes.

I remembered that when I was getting a quote for some building work at home. Several builders from different sized firms came round to look at the job. One really stood out for me. Instead of just giving me a price for the work, he made relatively detailed sketches and included energy-saving tips like cutting back on certain spotlights and rearranging them so we would need fewer of them. He really went into detail, and it felt like he was already working on our project. I took that concept and adapted the process to our digital marketing and web design service. Our larger competitors went into the pitch with slick presentations about themselves and how good they were. We did away with all that and put the client first. We would invest and do a full audit of their website, how it could be improved for search engines and redesigned for better user experience. We would even go as far as asking our designer to mock-up of a redesigned website, showing how the client could improve their website along with the full audit. This not only gave the client the feeling that they were already working with us, but it also showed them we were willing to provide value upfront.

We got so good at pitching using this technique that we almost always won the client. This formed the basis for us winning larger clients and building the business to a million-pound turnover agency in just a few years. All this came from drawing inspiration from the builder who came to quote for a job at my home.

29

HANDLING FAILURE AND SUCCESS

When people look at a business from the outside they see it in very simple terms: success or failure. In reality, being a successful parent in business is a long journey of constantly overcoming challenges, fighting fires, and finding new ways to increase efficiency and profitability. You'll experience a rollercoaster of emotions, but the extreme highs and lows of starting and running a business, as well as juggling being a good parent, are what makes entrepreneurship both exciting and scary.

From failure to success

How you handle these extremes is one of the keys to succeeding in the long run. One thing I want to point out about failure and success is that, in reality, failure doesn't come until you give up for good, because you will 'fail' at something every single day in business. Either way, I don't label it as failure, I just call it a challenge. You won't fail if you overcome the challenge, and when you overcome it, it becomes a success.

Turning around what might have been considered a failure and making it a success, perhaps in a different form, is known as a 'pivot'.

The key here is to programme your mind into not labelling something as a success or failure, instead, focus just on overcoming challenges and making progress. Accept the fact that things will not always go to plan, prepare yourself and get into the right emotional and mental state to overcome any obstacles that get in the way of reaching a goal. Look at success as a series of milestones, break down these milestones into short bursts of activities and tasks. All of those smaller milestones lead to the big goal at the end (See chapter 8 for more on this).

QUICK STORY

When I and others invested in an app start-up business called Gurooo, we knew it was going to be a difficult journey. I was used to running service-based businesses, so this was unchartered territory for me. Whilst we were experienced in building and developing technology for other businesses and charging them for it as a service, Gurooo was a technology product that needed to bring in revenue itself.

When one of the investors pulled out due to some challenges he was experiencing in his own business, we were left with a huge budget deficit. It meant that we couldn't fully develop the app to the extent where it was ready for mass market. It also meant that we had to close down the business unit.

On the face of it, the start-up venture was a failure. However, what happened in the following years turned around the whole situation. As I moved on to focus on my consultancy business, I eventually met a company based in the Far East who asked us to develop an app very similar to Gurooo, to be used internally for their engineers. We had already developed 60 per cent of what they wanted, so we utilised our existing experience and code base to build their new app. What was originally deemed a failure turned into a success, because we re-used our experience, knowledge and assets in a different business model, and I recouped some of my investment.

It turned out to be a pivotal moment in the business. We realised that we were really good at turning concepts and ideas from entrepreneurs and businesses into reality, and we were able to build and develop the technology that they wanted. We just weren't very good at monetising the technology itself. I added custom technology development to the service offering of my digital marketing consultancy. We could take a crazy idea from a business or entrepreneur, build it and deliver a totally bespoke system or piece of technology. Today my clients come to me with all kinds of weird and wonderful ideas. Had I not invested in and started Gurooo, and at least tried to build something, I wouldn't have become known for technology development.

What others called a failure all those years ago when we didn't manage to achieve the original goal, turned into a new opportunity and a whole new business model.

Another pivot, involving a much more well known brand, is the story behind YouTube. Today, it's hard to imagine that YouTube was anything but a highly successful video streaming platform, home to billions of videos that people and businesses around the world upload every second of the day.

However, not many people know that YouTube was originally started as a video-based dating service, where people looking for a partner match could upload a video describing their ideal partner and also browse videos from other people. Over time, the service slowly pivoted and turned into a platform for all kinds of weird and wonderful videos, which eventually lead to Google's $1.65 billion acquisition, which in those days was a huge acquisition for a technology company.

Learn from the challenges

It's been said that every challenge is an opportunity in disguise – a bit corny maybe, but very true. Business is just a long road of challenges and hurdles. Overcome these and you level up. You become a more experienced, wise and resilient entrepreneur.

In order to learn from the challenges, you have to accept the fact that things won't always go to plan and that the road ahead in business isn't a smooth journey. There is most definitely an opportunity after every single challenge you overcome – you just have to look out for it.

After the failure of the Gurooo app, I pivoted and turned it into a technology development business. This proved to be a great learning experience for me. I have been involved in other new technology ventures since then, but I am now self-aware enough to know that I can deliver the technology and even the marketing of such ventures, but I would need a strong commercial partner to help take the whole thing to market.

The challenges in your business help you understand and learn more about your own strengths and weaknesses, where you should focus your efforts and when to bring in other skill-sets to help you deliver a business model.

30

DEALING WITH STRESS AND PRESSURE

When you're constantly dealing with challenges and fighting fires in business it can really start to take its toll on your physical and mental health, and on your relationships. Over a long period of time, stress can present itself in ways you wouldn't expect, and it can do long-term damage if it is not recognised and managed.

Along with business-related stress, as a parent entrepreneur you also need to factor in the chaos of family life and raising kids – the daily grind of school runs, tantrums and other child-related issues. All this stress can really tip you over the edge if you don't recognise it and put measures and processes in place to help you manage your physical and mental health.

It's not unusual as a parent entrepreneur to feel like you're to blame in some way when things don't go to plan, and this in turn causes stress. You might feel stressed when things aren't moving quickly enough or don't pan out. If your business or staff aren't performing, you might feel responsible and put pressure on yourself to sort it out, because it's your business after all. If the kids aren't behaving or an accident has happened at home, you might blame yourself for not giving them enough attention or for not having the foresight to be able to prevent these tantrums or accidents from happening in the first place. The truth is, even with the best planning and foresight, things will almost certainly go wrong at some point. The impact these stresses have on you will depend on how you view these challenges.

It's possible to learn to control stress by self-regulating and examining your thoughts or emotions, and the way you react when things don't go to plan or whenever there is a crisis situation. First of all you have to get to the bottom of the real reason why pressure and stress occurs. Really understanding why you feel stressed in itself will solve much of the problem.

QUICK STORY

During a stressful period whilst I was setting up multiple businesses after I sold my digital marketing agency, I started to get anxiety and panic attacks. I was clearly taking on too much at the time and I recognised that something had to be done about the way I was handling it mentally.

I created what I called a 'Stress Calender'. It was a seperate calender that I set up on my phone for periods of stress or anxiety. I would write down bullet points on the calender explaining what I was stressed about on that particular day and set a reminder for each year, who I was getting pressure from and possible solutions that were available to solve it. Just writing it down made me feel better because it laid down the whole situation in a bullet point format for me to see from a birds eye view. In many cases the source of the pressure wasn't even external, it was just me giving myself pressure and the solution was often already there, I just needed time to execute it. After talking to friends about it, I realised that many of our stresses are often caused by ourselves and that anxiety is brought about because of the standards that we set ourselves.

The 'Stress Calender' achieved two things for me; it helped me see the stressful situation for what it really was, in the most part me putting pressure on myself which was causing the anxiety. It also helped me document these stressful periods. I still add to the 'Stress Calender' now, and as I look back at things I was stressed about a month or a year ago it puts everything in persepctive. What was a stressful situation a year ago is just another memory and another challenge that I overcame and learned from.

> **"EVERYTHING YOU'RE STRESSED AND WORRIED ABOUT TODAY WON'T EVEN A MATTER A YEAR FROM NOW."**

In chapter 9, I wrote about the importance of planning for those unexpected crisis moments - when things happen beyond your control and affect your plans. If you have sufficient back-up plans in place when these scenarios happen, you won't feel stressed, because you have the confidence to know that plans can still go ahead.

As a parent, you'll probably be all too familiar with what can happen if you don't plan ahead. Not taking enough spare underwear when your child is potty training, or forgetting to bring snacks and drinks when you're out and about can cause all sorts of havoc. You only have to have one nightmare incident to know how important it is to be prepared for every eventuality. It's exactly the same in business. If you develop the mindset of overcompensating and planning for all eventualities that you can think of, you can avoid most stressful and pressured situations.

If the source of stress is running out of something, such as time (you might be on a tight deadline) or money (an issue with cash flow), then having a back-up plan B, or even plan C, in place will almost always solve this. In fact, running out of time or money are two of the main causes of stress for most entrepreneurs. Always factor in too much of both when planning for a new project.

When you have a plan B or even plan C, you will feel more in control and less stressed.

Perhaps you feel stressed because you are overworked and feel overwhelmed by the amount of work piling up. This might be a sign that you need to scale up your business. (For more on how to scale up your business through technology, outsourcing or hiring more staff, see chapter 33). It's important to remember when running a business that you simply can't do everything. There will come a point when you need other people, systems, processes or technology to help you manage and operate different parts of your business. If you have too much work on, you need to break down your list of tasks and actions, and you need to either delegate to staff, outsource some of the work or utilise technology to automate some of those tasks. Having too much work is a sure sign that your business is growing and you are developing to the next stage.

Managing customer expectations is also a must, because you can't action every single request from every customer or client at the same time. If you are in a service-based business, manage expectations by telling your customers an expected timescale for delivering the work. If you are a product-based business, again, manage expectations from the outset by explaining expected delivery time.

Are you pushing yourself too hard?

If you are feeling overwhelmed with work you have to be super honest with yourself, and ask yourself this: who is giving you that pressure? Is it your clients and customers, your staff, your family, or deep down is it you giving yourself a hard time because you have set the bar so high that you are struggling to meet your own expectations? Most of the time it will just be you giving yourself a hard time.

External pressures are a given in business, but they can be managed. It's more difficult to manage yourself and your own expectations. Train and programme your brain to find the balance between working hard and working smart. Working hard is doing everything yourself and taking all accountability for everything in your business. Working smart is finding and filtering out the tasks and actions that can be done by others, without it affecting your profit line too much.

QUICK STORY

Sometimes the problem is what you make it to be. Quite often the solutions to your stress, pressures and challenges are already there in your head – you already know the answer, but your mind can become so clouded that you can't see the solution through all the other thoughts.

A good friend of mine who coaches business leaders and high-level executives once gave me an analogy involving a glass of muddy water. If you shake the glass and keeping swirling it around, the water becomes even more cloudy and muddy. The same is true when you are trying to solve a problem – you keep thinking and thinking about it, and running dozens of combinations and scenarios in your head. The more you think about it, the more confused your mind becomes. But if you just stop swirling and shaking the glass, after a short while, all the mud and sediment will settle at the bottom of the glass, and the water at the top becomes clear.

When you are stressed and have too much on your mind, take yourself out of the situation and do something else, preferably something totally different and relaxing. You'll be surprised how quickly a solution, that was probably in your head all along, floats to the top of your mind.

There are times when you might feel stressed, sad or just down about the situation you're in. In both business and parenting, it's normal to experience times when you feel like nothing's going the way you want it to, you feel stressed because you don't think you're making progress or you simply don't feel the people around you are being supportive. This is totally normal.

During times like these, try to change your sense of perspective. Take a step back and think about your current situation. Don't focus on the things you *haven't* got, think about everything you *have* got – your family, your business and the fact that you're actually running it yourself. Think about all the really hard times you've been through, and come out the other side of. Give yourself a big pat on the back for how far you've come, for what you've already achieved, and for surviving being a parent! Accept that things might not be going your way right now, but take the time to have a glass of wine, go for a run and burn off some energy, or have a rest – tomorrow's a new day with new opportunities, you'll be just fine.

31

UNDERSTAND WHEN IT'S TIME TO REST

There is so much on social media from influencers and business celebrities about working long hours and pushing yourself to the limit in order to succeed, that it leads even the most ambitious of individuals to question if they are working hard enough.

I agree with not wasting any time. I agree with using up any dead time to be productive and add value to your business. I also agree that in order to succeed in business you need to sacrifice a few things. But sometimes the message about not wasting time can be mistranslated and can come across as 'Don't sleep and don't rest if you want to succeed'. I think long hours and sacrifice are to be expected when starting or running a business in its early years, but not at the expense of your health. You need to make sure that you have the energy to function as a parent too.

> **RECOGNISE THAT RESTING IS A BIG PART OF BEING SUCCESSFUL IN BUSINESS.**

It's very easy to look at successful individuals in business and try to mimic their success by following the way they succeeded – but you are not them and you never will be. The important thing here is to understand what *your own* strengths and weaknesses are, how and when *you* perform the best, and doubling down during those times. Not everyone can survive on a few hours of sleep, be a parent to their kids, and then go off and run a business. You might be able to do that for a short period of time but it's not a good way to live long-term. You need to understand your own limits and to what extent you can push yourself and, most importantly, recognise when it's time to rest.

QUICK STORY

I'm actually writing this chapter having just recovered from a pretty bad virus that took ages to clear. I am hardly ever ill, but this time it really took me by surprise and I ended up having quite a bit of downtime. This was due to a combination of not resting when my body was telling me to, not eating properly and generally not looking after myself. I had been working on a new project with some new investors and trying to turn things around quickly so I was working around the clock and not paying attention to the signals that my body was giving off, telling me that I needed to slow down and rest. Finally nature caught up with me and stopped me right in my tracks, meaning I was out of action for three weeks. Looking back now it just wasn't worth it because in the long run the illness has set me back.

I realise that a big part of being successful in anything is recognising when you're tired, no longer productive or adding value. Working hard and not wasting time are important, but when you're absolutely shattered you're not going to be very productive, and you certainly won't be giving your best. The most productive thing to do is actually rest and recharge. Getting enough rest, eating healthily and recharging your batteries are actually really important. If you factor these things into your day you will find that your brain is sharper, you will make better decisions, and work in a more productive and smarter way.

Value-added rest

There are some days when instead of working quickly and going a hundred miles an hour, I stop, take a walk, play with my kids or even just take the dog out for a stroll, only to return much clearer on my objectives for the day. There is a difference between being lazy and resting because your body needs it. I like to call this 'Value-Added Rest' – you're resting because your work will benefit from it. It's a planned rest, and if you factor this type of rest into your day you will find you are more productive during your push periods.

When you're working long hours and trying to balance running a business with being a parent, this can add to the stress and tiredness. Being a parent entrepreneur means you must also factor in time with your family as part of your business plans too.

If you have young kids, expecting to work 100 per cent of the time on your business is just not reasonable. To keep a healthy balance you need to spend time with your family too. Factor in family time as a part of your Value-Added Rest. Use it to recharge and re-evaluate your goals for the day in your mind. After all, what are you working so hard for if it's not for the benefit of your family?

During the planning of my days, weeks or months, I often purposely factor in escaping the office for a few hours to pick up my kids from school and then take them for a treat, or if the weather is good use this as an excuse to go to the park. It's a treat for them and it's rest for me, and it also helps me to clear my mind and put some things in perspective. This is especially helpful when my day or week hasn't been going as well as I'd have wanted it.

Learn to be aware of your own strengths and weaknesses, learn from what successful people are doing and take some tips, but don't try to mimic what they're doing exactly. Understand how your own brain and body works – push yourself by all means and sometimes even past your limits – but make sure you understand when you're pushing too far or too often, and know when to stop, take a rest and recharge.

32

MANAGE EVERYONE AROUND YOU

Running a smooth business is mostly about how you manage everything that surrounds your great product or service. It's about managing the expectations of everyone from your wife, husband or partner, to your kids, your staff, your customers, partners and investors. A smooth-running business has people and processes in place to ensure everything works as efficiently as possible. When you have this, you can then scale up. It's not just about being profitable, it's about having everything in place so you can grow and scale your business. In order to do this you have to manage many different levels of people.

Managing your wife, husband or partner

If you are starting a new business whilst being a parent, you'll be spending every single waking hour outside of being a parent on your business, and if not you'll be thinking about it all the time. When you are splitting your life between work and family, it's very easy to forget about your wife, husband or partner. Managing this relationship throughout each stage of starting and running your business will keep it strong.

Make sure you bring your partner into your vision. Explain what your goals and expectations are, what the expected timelines, timescales and milestones look like, and the time you will need to spend at each stage. More importantly, make sure they know how you are going to allocate your time, so that they still get some of your time and attention too.

By talking your partner through your plan, it shows them that you care for and respect them, it sets down your expectations and it allows them to align theirs with yours. It also allows them to plan their own life so that they can help you focus on your business.

QUICK STORY

Throughout my business journey, my wife hasn't been directly involved in the day-to-day operations of my businesses, but she has been involved in the bigger picture of how we can make our lifestyle work for the family. We've worked hard at aligning both my expectations of my businesses and family life, and her expectations of family and her work. When it comes down to simple things like school runs, ballet classes, swimming lessons or violin lessons she knows that there will be many times when she will take the kids. She also knows that when I can take the kids, and give her a break, I will. This mutual and unspoken understanding is set because I managed expectations right from the beginning.

There have been many times in my technology businesses where I have suddenly had to leave the dinner table because of a major server outage in order to make sure the system gets back up so our clients don't get affected. There are times when we are on holiday, when we might be on beach and I have had to take a call with an investor or a client because something big has happened. Because I laid down the expectations from the start, my wife knows that if I have to take a call or suddenly leave the dinner table in the middle of a family dinner, it's because there is an emergency, and that I wouldn't go unless it was just that.

She also knows that when I can, I will take time off work to be with the kids, pick them up from school or take them out, so she can have some time with her friends.

Managing your kids

When it comes to being a parent entrepreneur, managing the expectations of your kids is as important as managing those of your partner. Kids will always want to play, they don't understand urgency, priority or the fact that if you didn't go to work all the time they wouldn't be able to have the life they do.

From an early age, I explained to my kids that mums and dads need to work to be able to give them a good life, to be able to buy them the toys that they have, to be able to go on holidays or trips and to be able to live in the house that they do. They also knew that I worked long hours and even after they went to bed. On the flip side I made sure they knew that when it came to things like parents' evening, Christmas nativity, school fairs or dance shows, I would move my work schedule so that I could be there.

With kids it's a little trickier to align your expectations because they may not fully understand what you're telling them. The key thing here is to let them know that you may work long hours, but you are willing to make it up by allocating dedicated times of the week just for them. During those allocated times it's imperative that you really do focus on them and put work to one side. By planning this time into your business schedule, it means that not only are you giving them the attention that they deserve, it's also giving you a break away from the business to recharge your mind too.

Managing clients and customers

In the early years of a business it's very easy to over-promise, just to please new customers and clients. You want them to know you can deliver more than your competitors can, so you win and keep their business.

Offering your customers more value than anyone else and going that extra mile is a great strategy to build your business. This is especially the case in service-based businesses or when customer service is an extremely important part of your product offering. This can make the difference between a customer leaving and going to a competitor, or one that stays with you, continues to buy from you and even refers their friends and colleagues. Whilst this is a great strategy, it's important to set expectations from the outset, so that your customers understand that the extra mile *really is* the extra mile and not part of the original product or service. This is important because when customers get used to that extra mile, it might seem that you're not delivering as much when you cut down that additional value, when in fact you're delivering exactly what you said you would.

Set expectations and boundaries with customers and clients in a tangible, measurable way. Let's say you sell a product as part of a new client promotion, and you give them an additional 10 per cent off as a goodwill gesture. Make sure it's clear the extra 10 per cent is not part of the original product. If you are giving some of your product away for free, package it up separately and differently so they know it's an additional promotion and not part of their additional order.

If you are running a service-based business you are probably selling time or tasks. Sometimes time- and task-based services aren't as tangible or measurable as product-based businesses. If you are giving more time or additional tasks for free as part of a client promotion, you need to make sure your clients are aware they are getting more than they ordered. In this case, you can add the extra time or tasks to the invoice and mark them as FREE, Complementary or just zero. When the customer sees it, they know that you have added something extra but not charged for it. This then feels more like you added something to your service rather than just extended their original service.

QUICK STORY

In the early days, I used to go way above and beyond my service remit. I was the go-to guy for web and marketing tasks. Clients called me at all hours of the day and began to take it for granted that I would always be available. They continued to call me even in the evening or late at night to ask questions or to ask me to look into something for them. This was great for building the business, as my clients slowly started to rely on me and gave me more and more work. But over time this became unscalable – I wasn't resting in the evening and it felt like I was constantly chasing after tasks and projects. The problem was, if I suddenly stopped answering my phone, the clients would think I wasn't responsive enough. In the end I decided, instead of not answering the phone at all, I would put an out-of-hours surcharge on any tasks or queries that would come after normal office hours. The surcharge wasn't ridiculous, but it was more than my usual rate, so when clients saw this they would think twice about if they really needed to speak to me in the evening, or just wait until the next day. If the task still came in during the evening, at least I was charging more for it. This helped me manage the expectations of my clients in those early years.

Managing your staff and team

When you get to the stage where you start hiring employees, it can be very exciting. You want to make sure they are happy and don't leave, especially if they are good employees. As you are still a small business, things might be casual and you don't want to be over formal with the HR side of things in case you scare off your staff. However, as you grow you don't want your business culture to become too casual to the point where there is no structure. You want everyone in your team to adhere to the same set of rules.

Setting expectations early with your team is a sure-fire way to scale up much more easily later on in your journey. When your new team members start, as part of the contract signing and induction into their job role, you might want to set down some ground rules that everyone, including yourself, will follow – after all, just like parenting, leading by example is the best way to ensure people follow the rules.

In the early days, you might need your new team members to do a little more than expected from time to time. This is where the mutual expectation and respect begins. There might be times when you need them to go above and beyond their own roles, such as staying a little later to meet a deadline. Whilst this might already be in their employment contract, it's always good to talk through it in person so that they understand there will be times they will need to stay late to hit deadlines, but only when necessary. In return you should expect to give them some leeway too. There may be times when something unexpected comes up and they need to come in slightly later, or if they have a dentist appointment that they didn't book in on time, you might want to allow it.

The idea here is that you need to set down the ground rules, but be flexible with your team's needs – they will also reciprocate and give you more if they already know what to expect. Sometimes it's the unspoken expectations and respect for each other that builds a strong team culture.

Managing your business partner

When you decide to start a business with a partner, it's important that you plan and discuss the vision for the business, what it means to each of you, how it might grow, and what the milestones and goals will be, from the outset. It can be extremely exciting and rewarding to work together like this, but whilst you might share the same vision for the business, your visions of what you each want to get out of it might differ slightly.

You personally might want to build the business to the point where you don't need to work as much, so you can spend more time with your family and dip in and out of the business. Your partners may wish to build the business to a point where it can be acquired by a larger company, with the partners becoming part of a corporate management team. Other partners might want to get the business to a certain point, sell it and retire.

If all the partners set out their personal goals within the business plan, it paints a clear picture and aligns everyone's expectations of each other. Having this understanding in place can save a lot of stress later on in the life of the business, when it is much bigger with a more complicated structure. When you first partner up in business, it can be a friendly affair, but as the business grows there is more to lose. The stress and challenges of running a much larger business can start to have an effect on that friendship. By understanding each other's goals from the outset, everyone knows where they stand.

Managing your friends

I've talked about the different kinds of friends in chapter 20, but generally your social life is usually put on the back burner for a long period of time when you start up a business and this can have an impact on friendships. You can only turn down an invite for casual drinks or dinner so many times before it affects the way that person sees you as a friend. It's true that if they are a genuine friend, they won't mind this, but when it happens over a long period of time, it can seem like you are distancing yourself from them when in fact all you're trying to do is have a balanced life between family and business.

Sit down with your close friends and take them through what you're planning to do. Let them know that you expect to be very busy juggling work and family, but will try to make an effort and show your face at social events and occasions when you can. This is often all that's needed to set the expectations for your closest friends. It also shows them that you respect them, and that you care enough about your relationship to explain to them that your life is about to change and you are working hard towards a goal. Reassure them that they are an important part of your life.

If some of your friends also have families, this makes things much easier. Many of my friends now have their own families and their kids are also the same age as mine, so we often merge family time with catching up with friends. Our kids play together and the parents can get together as a social occasion. Over the years this has become the norm, and now the majority of my social circle revolves around friends whose kids are also friends of our kids.

Keep everyone's best interests at heart

The main thing to remember when managing different groups of people and processes is that at the end of the day, you have everyone's best interests in mind. Whether it's your partner, kids, customers, business partner or staff, as long as you manage their expectations and align them with yours, family and business life can go much more smoothly than if you didn't communicate any of your expectations right from the start.

33

SCALING YOUR BUSINESS

Before you can start to scale your business up, you need to make sure you really understand every part of it. As a new business owner, you have to wear all kinds of hats: sales, marketing, operations, finance, accounts and sometimes even cleaning toilets if needs be. Whilst juggling so many different types of tasks and skillsets might be difficult, understanding each function and its contribution to the overall success of your business will be the key to scaling up in a structured way.

That's not to say you have to be good at all of these job functions – you can't be good at everything and if you want to grow your business you don't have time to learn – but you do need to understand what's involved in those job functions.

Knowing when to hire staff

In the beginning you will be doing everything yourself, but as you get more customers or clients, and revenue or investment starts to build, you need to focus your time on the tasks that are going to help push the business forward. If you hire staff too early you'll waste precious resources, and if you hire too late you'll waste time scaling up your business.

When you've already worked a 9 to 5 job for a long time, then suddenly become your own boss, it can feel natural to continue the mindset of being in a job in the day-to-day operations. However, to be successful in business in the long-term, you need go from working *in* it to working *on* it. That means not just focusing on selling your product or providing a service, but eventually delegating all those jobs to others so you can focus on the more strategic parts of your business - planning new product and service lines, growing the business and plotting out the future.

There's no exact science to timing when to hire staff, but the moment you feel that you are bursting at the seams with work and all those hats you are wearing are just not helping your business grow, that's the time to think about getting someone to assist you. Depending on what type of business you have, you might be able to outsource some job functions. Outsourcing allows you to test the waters and slowly release some of the pressure from your day-to-day operations without the long-term commitment of having to hire full-time staff, where you have to deal with payroll, insurance or pensions, and HR. If outsourcing doesn't work out the way you expect, you can just take back that function and cancel the outsourcing.

Deciding which tasks to delegate

So you've decided that letting go and delegating or outsourcing some of the tasks is a good idea, but which ones? At first you might feel that all the roles in your business are important, after all they each contribute something. The tasks that you truly excel at, keep. Keep the tasks that bring the most value and revenue too. You can't afford to lose revenue, so outsourcing this completely could affect your survival (it's fine to outsource the parts of it that take up the most time).

QUICK STORY

When my business partner and I were growing our digital marketing agency, he would bring in the business and I would service it. My business partner took care of everything on the business development front: marketing, cold calling, setting up appointments and doing the pitches. I provided the entire service, from design to web development, Search Engine Optimisation (SEO) to digital marketing. As we got more and more new clients, I had didn't have enough time to service them, so we outsourced some of the design and web development to freelancers. We kept the SEO and digital marketing in-house because that's where our retained revenue came from. The quality of that work had a direct impact on whether or not clients stayed with us. As we got bigger, we brought the design and web development back in-house and hired staff to take care of those functions. As we continued to grow we hired more digital marketers. Slowly I stepped back from the day-to-day operations of working on clients' projects and my role was to develop processes, reporting and ways to improve my team and their output of work, so that we could get even bigger clients. By the time I sold and exited the agency we had 15 staff and recurring client revenues of £1 million – the business had grown by outsourcing the right parts.

In the property development business we took outsourcing even further. We would outsource entire functions of our property portfolio. At one point we had over £50 million of residential and commercial properly in development (around 350 apartments across the UK, all at different stages of planning and construction) managed by just three of us. All the important functions were project managed in-house, whilst all the technical, engineering and planning was outsourced.

In fact, for any new business that I start now, I will always outsource a large portion of the job functions first to prove a business case, before hiring a full-time team to take reigns.

Using technology to scale up

Today, technology can play a vital role in scaling up your business at speed in the most cost-effective way. Technology can allow you to not only be a better businessperson, but also a better parent. Synchronising your business operations and family schedule in the cloud can help you to have a better picture of what's going on in all aspects of your life.

Whilst you might be hands on and physically able to tend to both business and family initially, there will come a time when being able to manage your business remotely will not only make life easier, but may be essential for you to succeed as a parent in business.

Find the technology that fits your business and family lifestyle, and build the tools and processes into your business, so that gradually you can still run your business remotely at the same level of quality.

Technology is constantly changing and providing new ways to speed up processes and make life simpler. Regardless of what the technology is and how far it has come in its integration into our lives, the key here is to adopt the technology that will help you scale your business and family life. You don't need to adopt everything that's out there, just the parts that will speed things up, save money, streamline processes, and most importantly, help you spend more and better quality time with your family.

Of course for some businesses working in the cloud, 100 percent isn't going to be possible, particularly with bricks and mortar businesses. But even for these types of businesses, parts could be monitored or operated remotely with staff input. Whilst you might think you have to constantly monitor your staff physically, simply changing your own perception of what it is you have hired them to do can change the way you assess their work. Use cloud systems to track the progress of all of your staff by asking them to document their work throughout the day on a cloud system that you can access via your laptop or phone.

I cover this in more detail in chapter 10 but I use cloud project management tools to communicate with all of my teams, partners and clients who are spread out across different time zones. We rely on these cloud platforms to be able to run individual tasks, projects and entire businesses without physically being there all the time. Being able to remotely manage my business most of the time means I have more freedom when it comes to my family.

34

WHAT DOES SUCCESS LOOK LIKE TO YOU?

Success can mean something completely different to each individual, and your version of success will be unique to your own circumstances.

There's no exact blueprint to being a parent in business, but in this book we've covered techniques in discovering what it is you want to achieve, how to overcome challenges, the real reason you want to achieve them and how you go about achieving them.

Money and being your own boss are usually the misunderstood reasons for starting your own business, but in reality, money and being your own boss are just the results, not the reasons. For many of you who picked up this book, what might have appealed to you the most is probably the journey of a parent in business, rather than JUST the journey of being a parent or JUST the journey of starting a business.

For many of you, building your own business and scaling it to the point where you can have the freedom to genuinely enjoy time with your family, without it affecting your career or earnings, is the reason for embarking on this rewarding journey.

For me, I wanted to see my kids grow up. I wanted to be there for every parents evening, I wanted to be there for every play and nativity and I wanted to have the freedom to be able to just pick up and go somewhere with them any day of the week, whenever I wanted, without it having any impact on my career or my earnings. I didn't want to have to take days off work or ask for permission from my boss to take my kids to the dentist. I didn't want my wage to be affected if I suddenly wanted to take my family on a last-minute holiday. I wanted the freedom to be able to just take my wife out for lunch whilst the kids were at school without any planning. For a long time I thought it was the dream of having more money that made me want to succeed in business. But after so many years of running businesses, overcoming challenges and missing out on key milestones with my kids, I realised that the real reason I wanted to be successful in business was because I wanted to be successful as a parent.

I hope that you've enjoyed following my journey as a parent entrepreneur and that some of my thoughts have resonated with you. I also hope that this book has given you the tools and confidence you need to take the plunge and set up on your own, prepared for the many challenges and rewards of being a parent in business.

I wish you all the very best as you embark on your own journey to become a successful parent entrepreneur.

Printed in Great Britain
by Amazon

41468053R00149